lol...OMG!

lol...
OMG!

What Every Student Needs to Know
About Online Reputation Management, Digital
Citizenship and Cyberbullying

MATT IVESTER

SERRA KNIGHT
PUBLISHING

004.678

IVE

Published by Serra Knight Publishing
955 S. Virginia St., Suite 116, Reno, NV 89502

Readers should be aware that Internet websites offered as citations and/or sources for further information may have changed or disappeared between the time this was writ-ten and when it is read.

Limit of Liability/Disclaimer of Warranty: While the publisher and author have used their best efforts in preparing this book, they make no representations or warranties with respect to the accuracy or completeness of the contents of this book and specifi-cally disclaim any implied warranties of merchantability or fitness for a particular purpose. No warranty may be created or extended by sales representatives or written sales materials. The advice and strategies contained herein may not be suitable for your situation. You should consult with a professional where appropriate. Neither the publisher nor author shall be liable for any special, incidental, consequential, or other damages.

Library of Congress Cataloging-in-Publication Data

Ivester, Matt.
   Lol...omg! : what every student needs to know about online reputation management, digital citizenship and cyberbullying / Matt Ivester.
     p. cm.
   ISBN 978-0-615-52889-2 (hardback)
   1. Personal information management. 2. Online identities. 3. Online social networks – Safety measures. 4. Online social networks – Social aspects. 5. Internet and youth. 6. Cyberbullying. I. Title.
   HQ799.9.I58I94 2011
   004.6780842—I94   2011914953

Printed in the United States of America
FIRST EDITION
9 8 7 6 5 4 3 2 1

OCT 1 8 2011

To my family, who have always loved and supported me

Contents

lol...
OMG!

Foreword

BY DAVID BOHNETT

Matt Ivester has written a guide to the opportunities and dangers of social networks and online behavior that will not only save reputations but literally save lives. This book will help a great many people. Matt has been at the forefront of the digital age for years. He is a responsible citizen who has learned much from his own entrepreneurial experiences, and, to our great benefit, he has used that knowledge to create this important work.

There are many hazards and pitfalls of life online. The material that Matt presents in a thoughtful and articulate manner needs to become standard curriculum in our schools. He encourages us all to forge identities online that are consistent with our better selves, and to take a proactive stance on creating and monitoring our online image.

Matt clearly explains the notion of a permanent record, an idea that ought to strike fear in all of us. What we say and do online, the pictures we post, the tweets we send, the blogs we write and the blithe comments we make about ourselves and others will be available to the world forever. Forever for anyone to see, current and future spouses, potential employers, parents, teachers, and even law enforcement. Matt takes all of these matters into account and offers sound advice as to how to cope with the demands and responsibilities of life in the digital age.

Most important, Matt addresses the issue of cyber-bullying, a dangerous and sometimes lethal aspect of our new digital environment. The anonymity and physical separation that the Internet affords have given birth to a new, insidious occupation, as people take refuge in the distance permitted by the Internet to disparage, embarrass and debase others.

The Internet was a very different place when I created GeoCities.com. The concept of user generated content was new and untested, and we had yet to develop any of the skepticism required for filtering the massive amount of content on the web.

My goal in creating GeoCities was to empower individuals online, to give them a voice and a space in the digital world where they could express themselves and connect with others of similar interests. From personal experience, I knew that there was a need to create a place where people could share their own thoughts and ideas, as well as to find comfort and strength in a group of like-minded digital citizens.

Matt's cautionary tale is important because we're on the verge of abusing our anonymity and freedom to the point that we undermine the very purpose of social networking and online individualism. Our actions have the power to compromise, as well as enhance, the myriad benefits of online community and social networking. Negative online attacks threaten the ability of sites with user-generated content to be safe escapes and channels for people to have their voices heard. As Matt explains in more detail in the coming pages, we must become conscious creators of content and take active responsibility for building our positive online reputations.

Near the end of this book, Matt addresses the idea of seeing ourselves, users of the Internet, as digital 'citizens' in a digital world. Let's all consider the kind of digital world in which we would want to be a citizen and how we can actively work toward creating and maintaining a useful and constructive digital space. Social networking is an incredibly powerful tool that is worth preserving. I encourage you to become empowered by the wisdom within Matt's book and to take an active role in forming a positive future for your digital world.

Preface

"The site was intended as a kind of Page Six for the varsity set, but it quickly grew into a malicious cesspool of barbs, disses, and insults."
Katie Couric, reporting on JuicyCampus.com

Four years ago, I created the biggest college gossip website in the country. It eventually became so out of control that student governments on various campuses were actually asking administrators to block access to the site, so that their students would stop using it. When I started it, though, I had never imagined the path that it would take.

I graduated from Duke University on May 15, 2005, without really knowing what I wanted to do for a job. Everyone around me, on the other hand, seemed to want to be a consultant; so, when I got an offer from a consulting firm, I took it. I was excited to be joining the working world, and, while I was there, I worked with amazing people and learned a lot about business. Perhaps the most important thing I learned, though, was that my

heart wasn't in consulting; I wanted to be able to imple-
ment my own ideas and watch them come to life. So, after
a little more than a year, I decided that I was ready to make
my mark on the world. I left my job and set out to start
my own company. Over the course of the next few years,
I would start several companies, some more successful
than others, but none more exciting, stressful, controversial,
public or popular than JuicyCampus.com.

JuicyCampus was, at its core, an anonymous (no login
required) message board organized by college campus.
Students could select their school, and then post a message on their campus's page, whether it be about a class
they were taking, a professor they liked or disliked, or some
juicy bit of gossip about a fellow classmate.

When I started the site I just wanted to create something
that lots of students would use. I thought that it would be
fun for students to have a place where they could read and
share the weird, amazing and hilarious things that happen
on campuses every day. I figured that people gossip offline
fairly harmlessly, so why not bring that gossip online? I
knew that some people might be temporarily embarrassed,
but I also thought, because these were college students and
not high schoolers, they would be able to brush off any
negative comments and move on without much ado. In
truth, I gave very little thought to what might happen, and
instead decided I would just give the idea a try and see if
it worked.

Our slogan was "Always Anonymous, Always Juicy," and
we encouraged students to "C'mon, give us the juice." And
they did. The site started off fairly innocuously – rumors

about who was dating whom, or the crazy stuff that happened at certain invite-only parties. Soon, though, it became a place where students posted intimate, and often offensive, remarks about their peers – including sexual histories, accusations of drug-use, and other salacious rumors. I expanded the site from the first seven campuses to more than sixty, confident that I could figure out a way to address student concerns. I wrote a letter called "Hate isn't Juicy," encouraging students to think carefully about what they were posting and how it might affect others. I hired employees, and we started removing threats of violence, contact information, and hate speech. Meanwhile, traffic on the site was going through the roof, and I was getting interview requests from huge news outlets like *People* and *The New York Times*. Investors offered me $1,000,000 to help grow the site, and for a short while, it felt like the site was a real success.

Unfortunately, as the site continued to grow, so did the problems associated with it. We received hundreds of distressed emails from students, parents and administrators. We also became the subject of two investigations by Attorneys General. The website had substantially deviated from my expectations. Online gossip wasn't the same as offline gossip, for a host of reasons. And my efforts to mitigate the damage simply weren't enough. The site was out of control, and, at 24, I simply didn't have the wherewithal or the experience to rein it in. I felt trapped, unable to simply shut the site down – I had employees counting on me for their livelihoods, and I had spent a lot of venture capital money with the expectation of a return on investment.

Luckily, life gave me a reset. In October 2008, we were running out of money and needed additional funding. That month, however, is when the economy really crashed. As a result, hardly anyone, and especially not controversial, pre-revenue gossip sites, was able to raise additional funding. So, on February 5, 2009, out of money, I shut down the site.

Now, with the renewed perspective that can only come from a few years of distance, I view JuicyCampus as what I would call an "lol...OMG!" I put the site up without much thought, and without a thorough understanding of the many important ways that online content differs from offline content. I just thought it would be fun (lol); but it quickly turned into something else – something much bigger, more negative, and harder to control than I had ever expected (OMG!).

I have been thinking about writing this book for years, because, unfortunately, and as will be illustrated by the examples and statistics in this book, the lol...OMG! phenomenon is not isolated just to me. It has become increasingly common, as putting up content online has quickly become incredibly easy, and education around how to think about that content has not kept up.

Several months ago, I was invited to speak as part of a panel called "Civil Discourse: Gossip, Bullying and the Digital Age." I was joined by a diverse group of panelists, spanning a wide range of experiences and expertise. We had a very open and honest conversation about the challenges facing college students today as a result of the quickly and constantly changing digital landscape. At the end of the panel's formal presentation, we opened up to questions from the audience. These questions demonstrated to me that online reputation management and cyberbullying are still serious concerns on college campuses – ones for which administrators and students alike are struggling to find answers. After that discussion, I realized that I had to finally write this book.

Upon my return home, I did a bit of research and found that there was a serious gap in the availability of educational materials on these topics geared toward higher education. There were many books on reputation management and personal branding focused on business professionals, and an abundance of information available about Internet safety and cyberbullying for children, but college students, for the most part, had been overlooked.

When I have discussed this issue with various people, from college administrators to Google executives, the consensus seems to be that funding is going toward younger students because we, as a society, are more protective of them, and kids are being exposed to technology at younger and younger ages. The thinking seems to be that by the time they get to college, they will be well-informed enough to make the right decisions, and they will understand what they are doing. I hope, and believe, that is right. Unfortunately, most of these programs are relatively new, and it will be years before the students benefitting from the full curriculum will arrive on college campuses. Moreover, I believe that education on the responsible use of technology needs to happen at every level, addressing the unique challenges that students face at all stages of their education.

I was part of the first class of graduating seniors from Duke University that had access to Facebook while still in school. Digital cameras were common at that point, but cameras in cell phones weren't nearly as pervasive as they are now. YouTube had launched only three months before my graduation and Twitter wouldn't arrive until nearly a year after. I am just barely on the cusp of the generation that has been affected by the boom in social media and digital technologies while still in college. That also means, however, that I am part of the first class of students experiencing the real-world ramifications of our digital decisions. Combine this with my JuicyCampus experience, and I realized that I was uniquely positioned to write a book like this: a guide to help students think about the way that they portray themselves, and the way that they treat others, online.

I know this book doesn't have all of the answers, but I do hope that it can be a platform upon which all of us can build.

CHAPTER 1

College in the Digital Age

"I'm talking about taking the entire social experience
of college and putting it online."
Jesse Eisenberg (as Mark Zuckerberg) in *The Social Network*

I honestly believe that college today is harder than it has been for any previous generation. I'm sure that many people would disagree. They might point to the advances that have been made in teaching methods, the increased availability of financial aid, the beautiful residence halls or even the extensive dinner buffets available on so many campuses nowadays. Almost certainly, though, the main reason for their disagreement would have to do with advances in technology, particularly the Internet. And in many respects they would be right.

Technology is completely changing the way that teachers teach and students learn – improving both exponentially. Once a second home for college kids, libraries are now relics of a bygone age. Today's students have access to virtually unlimited amounts of information with a simple search on Google. They can quickly ask their friends for homework help on Facebook, or they can crowd-source answers on sites like Quora, tapping into the collective knowledge of the online community. They can watch a how-to video on YouTube, or use Skype to practice their Mandarin directly with a student in China. They can take notes with a Livescribe smartpen and send those notes (audio and all) to a sick classmate with the click of a mouse. Lost the syllabus? Not a problem, because the professor has posted all of the course materials online. The amazing ways that technology has improved education could fill a book. But life on a digital campus doesn't mean all easy A's and smooth sailing. These recent technological advances have a dark side as well.

YOUR PERMANENT RECORD IS REAL

The idea of a "permanent record" used to be a myth used by school teachers to scare children into behaving, lest their bad deeds be written down in some alleged file that would haunt them forever. Now though, for better or worse, the permanent record is real, and has arrived in the form of the Internet. The mistakes that students make today, now easily searchable and immediately accessible, might *actually* haunt them forever.

College is a place to experiment, make mistakes, learn from those mistakes, and in the process, find yourself. Many college students are drinking alcohol for the first time, sharing their first romantic relationship, exploring their sexuality, and challenging their political and religious beliefs – all of which are an important part of growing up. But imagine if every one of your mistakes during this time was being captured and shared with everyone you know. Worse yet, imagine if those mistakes were shared with a complete stranger, or thousands of complete strangers; and not just shared today, but every day, for the rest of your life. Indeed, this is exactly what can happen if you are careless about your digital decisions. Many of today's students are finding themselves with a very real permanent record – one that reflects every poor decision of their youth, and is stored online forever.

Alarmingly, students are often their own worst enemies. They are the ones capturing their own mistakes and sharing them, without a second thought. At the time, they just don't realize that they are mistakes – errors in judgment that they may come to regret later in their lives. They post drunken pictures on Facebook, racially insensitive comments on blogs, and scandalous videos on YouTube. They do all of this without regard for who will see their content or how they will react, forgetting that the Internet is much more public, and more permanent, than other media.

When college students aren't broadcasting these things on their own, there are plenty of others willing to do it for them. The Internet has opened up new and more powerful avenues for bullies to torment their fellow students. Unfortunately, just as it provides lightning-fast access to research and easy communication with professors, it also provides a way to spread gossip, lies, embarrassing photos and videos, and other hurtful material at those same lightning speeds. Furthermore, it amplifies the power of the bully by enabling access to a global audience, and sometimes it provides a cloak of anonymity that makes the bully that much bolder and more brash. In this digital world, your permanent record isn't controlled by school administrators; anyone can write on it, including the bullies.

For years, the start of college had been an opportunity for students to reinvent themselves – a chance to start fresh with a new group of friends, and experiment with their identities. Today, most freshmen arrive on campus with a long digital trail. Their roommates have already Googled them, and they have already connected with many of their classmates on Facebook. Then, during their four years, the personal explorations, the missteps, and the learning opportunities of college life that once were private often become part of that permanent record, following them for years to come. The spotlight is on, and that's the part about going to college in the digital age that makes it tougher than ever before. Finding ways to take risks, experiment, and continue that crucial growing process without inhibition from the fear of everlasting repercussions is one of the greatest challenges facing students on college campuses today.

THE INTERNET ITSELF IS A COLLEGE STUDENT

Part of the reason that we are seeing issues of reputation management and cyberbullying on college campuses is that technology has developed at a faster pace than we can keep up with. Administrators and professors are still figuring out how to educate students about responsible use of emerging technologies, and Congress is still trying to figure out how to balance the extraordinary freedom provided by the Internet with its very real potential to harm.

For a college student, it may feel as if the Internet has been around forever. In fact, college campuses are just now getting their first "digital natives" – students who have never known a life without computers and the Internet. It's important to remember, though, that the Internet is actually still relatively new. While the technology that enables it has been around for much longer, it really didn't become popular until the mid-90's. That means the Internet is somewhere between 18 and 21 years old. As MIT professor and technology expert Sherry Turkle says in her book *Alone Together*, "Just because we grew up with the Internet, we think the Internet is all grown up." In

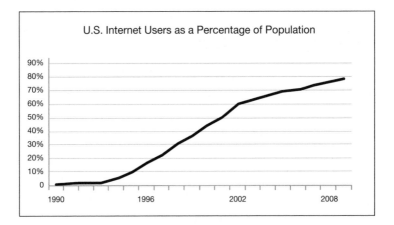

The Internet is only about 20 years old. Source: The World Bank, World Bank Development Indicators, Internet Users, Updated July 28, 2011

reality, though, it's still just the age of a college student, and in many ways is behaving like one.

The Internet is still finding itself. Entrepreneurs are pushing its boundaries, experimenting with new technologies. Engineers are helping it get stronger, faster and smarter. New websites pop up daily – some are tried out and then tossed aside, while others are kept to become part of the Internet's new identity. It's an exciting time for the Internet. But it's still a time of growth, and, as with any such time, there will be growing pains. So, just as administrators and professors are charged with shaping college students, all of us, the digital community, are charged with shaping the Internet. My intent in writing this book is to help students to do exactly that – not to tell you what is right or wrong, but to arm you with the information you will need to decide for yourself how these technologies should be used, and what being a good digital citizen means.

NOT-SO-COMMON COMMON SENSE

This book is written for college students and, to a certain degree, for high school students with college aspirations. It is intended to help you reflect more thoughtfully on how your online behavior might impact your day-to-day life. This book is not chock full of research or statistics about "digital natives"; in fact, most of the information is intuitive and common sense. However, when I talk to most college students and ask what key characteristics of the Internet make it different from the offline world, what questions they ask themselves before posting to their blogs, or what their privacy settings are on Facebook, more often than not, I get blank stares. And when I ask whether they've ever put up a picture or tweeted something that they wish they hadn't, they all say that they have. So, even though much of this may seem like common sense after you read it, it doesn't yet seem to have made its way into the collective common sense of today's college communities.

It's also important to note that this book doesn't have many easy answers. Once content you don't want out there is online, there's not much you can do about it. There are few real opportunities to "unpublish" or "unsend." I wish that I could offer an erase button, but I can't (and, in Chapter 3, I'll discuss why it is unlikely that Congress ever will either). But you can make a difference moving forward. This book isn't focused on what to do when something goes wrong – at that point a lot of the damage is already done, and, if it is enough damage, you may need to get lawyers involved if you want to do anything about it. Instead, this book focuses on how to prevent things from going wrong in the first place. It is meant to arm you with the resources to make educated decisions and to take deliberate actions online, becoming what I refer to as a conscious creator of content.

This book is broadly organized into three parts. The first part discusses the specific, fundamental ways that on-line is different from offline (Chapters 2 and 3). This lays the foundation that allows us to understand the issues that arise in the remainder of the book. The next part looks at the ways students represent themselves online, some of the consequences of their decisions, and some best practices to consider (Chapters 4-7). We then move into a discussion of how you, as students, treat one another online, again looking at potential consequences and offering some reflection questions (Chapters 8-10). Finally, I end by discussing the increasingly important role that a strong online reputation, built through conscious content creation and ethical digital citizenship, will play in all of our futures (Chapter 11).

CHAPTER 1: KEY TAKEAWAYS

– Technology has fundamentally changed college life in many positive ways, but also in some negative ways.

– College is a place to experiment and develop your identity, and making mistakes is a necessary part of that process. The challenge is to avoid having those mistakes captured and prevent them from haunting you forever.

– The Internet is only about 20 years old, and, much like a college student, its identity is still being shaped.

– There are no easy answers or quick fixes. The solution is to educate yourself and become a conscious creator of content, thinking about both how that content will reflect on you and how it might affect others.

CHAPTER 2

Sex, PowerPoint and Invasion of Privacy

"I feel embarrassed and humiliated...[I] never,
ever thought that these things would become public."
Paris Hilton, on the release of a private video

For any students who don't already know (and perhaps for the curious, but not-so-tech-savvy, parent or administrator who has picked up this book), "lol" and "OMG!" are acronyms commonly used in online communication. "Lol" stands for "laughing out loud," and "OMG!" stands for "Oh my God!" (or "Oh my gosh!"). I use them together to represent an increasingly common online phenomenon, in which students do something seemingly harmless and humorous online, only to later realize that what they've done is suddenly out of their control and having consequences they had never anticipated. Throughout the book, I explore several real-life examples of just such situations. In some instances, however, I change the subjects' names so as not to compound the effects of an already unfortunate situation. No other details have been changed, and when I do change the name, I note the change. So, with that said, we turn to the story of Melissa Murphy (name changed), a young woman whose joke, intended for just a few friends, turned into a nationwide glance into her sex life:

It was clever. And really well-written. Her friends thought it was hilarious. And it was sooooo juicy. It was every guy that Melissa Murphy had slept with in college, all laid out in a brilliant 42-page PowerPoint presentation. And these weren't just any guys – these were some of the hottest guys on campus – well-known athletes. It was a parody of a senior honors thesis, jokingly submitted to "The Department of Late Night Entertainment." She called it "An Education Beyond the Classroom: Excelling in the Realm of Horizontal Academics." In it, she provided detailed accounts of her sexual encounters with 13 of her classmates.

Each guy got a cover page with his name and pictures, followed by a slide that detailed how they had met, what they did in bed, and how the men performed. The highlights were captured in a section called "Memorable Moments." For example, Melissa noted how much she enjoyed when one of the men was "taking control, throwing me around like I weighed nothing, dominating me, grabbing my hair, switching positions rapidly." Not all of the reviews were positive, though – some were mean, others were incredibly embarrassing, and all of them were quite personal. She commented about one guy, "That gorgeous, perfect body of his was supporting a penile structure so disproportionately small that I had to take several deep breaths and force a smile…," and about another that, "His take on dirty talk was intensely amusing."

These excerpts are among the tamest of the text, which includes much more graphic and detailed commentary. At the end of each guy's section, Melissa gave him a score on a scale of one to 10. She explains at the end of the presentation that the men were evaluated based on Physical Attractiveness, Size, Talent, Creativity, Aggressiveness, Entertainment, Athletic Ability, and Bonus. She explains the Bonus section: "Bonus points were given for extraneous factors, such as the presence of an Australian accent and/or professional surfing skills. Points were deducted for rudeness or being Canadian." It was meant to be funny. And in many ways, it was; in fact, it was so funny that Melissa felt that it just had to be shared. Of course, it wasn't the sort of thing that she would want everyone to see, so she sent it to just three of her closest friends….

Melissa sent that email in May of 2010, and over the course of the next few months "The Duke Sex List," as it would come to be known, would go completely viral – first passed from one friend to another, then passed around fraternity lists, emailed all over the world, and finally catching the attention of the mainstream media. The story was picked up by the likes of *The New York Times*, *Vanity Fair*, and *The Today Show*. At the time of this book's publication, the simple blog post about it on Jezebel.com alone had received nearly 3,000,000 views. Melissa had never imagined that her little joke between friends (lol) would be seen by millions of people (OMG!). And the guys discussed in

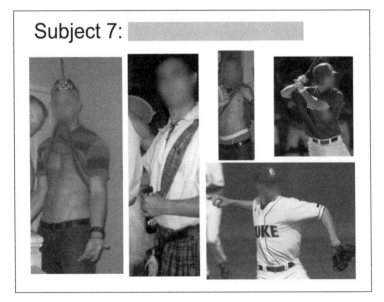

An education beyond the classroom: excelling in the realm of horizontal academics

Senior Honors Thesis
Duke University

Submitted to the Department of Late-Night Entertainment
in partial fulfillment of the requirements for a
Degree in Tempestuous Frolicking (D.T.F)

May, 2010

Subject 7:

Two slides from the now-infamous Duke Sex List

the PowerPoint certainly never did either. She told Jezebel, "I regret it with all my heart. I would never intentionally hurt the people that are mentioned on that."

Unfortunately, she did hurt them, and herself. For her "Subjects", as she called them, their personal lives were put on display. It was incredibly embarrassing for all of them – even those who got good reviews. Many of the press articles redacted their names, but not all of them. And now this PowerPoint has become part of their online identities – always there for a future employer, future date, future children, and so on, to find.

For the author, it's even worse. Google her real name and you get pages and pages of results filled with head-lines like, "Duke Coed's Scandalous Sex Ratings Go Viral" and "The Tragedy of [student's real name]." Some of the articles paint her as a "slut," while others celebrate her sexual liberation, but for the most part they all agree that her efforts were a showing of poor judgment. Dealing with this scandal caused her a great deal of humiliation, thousands of dollars in attorneys' fees (at one point the men were considering suing for invasion of privacy), and has permanently sullied her reputation online. There's no doubt that this will negatively affect what people will think of her, who will do business with her, and who will date her, among other things, for years to come.

What can we learn from this story? It's easy to be critical in retrospect. She should have never created it. She shouldn't have emailed it to anyone. Of course this was going to go viral. But in the moment of it all, you can be sure it wasn't so obvious. She didn't post it on a blog – she emailed it to a mere three friends. And she is otherwise a responsible and intelligent person – she graduated from one of the best universities in the country. She was just a college girl having some fun with her friends. While the specifics would be different for each of us, we're all susceptible to making this kind of mistake. And, as technology increasingly connects us, the likelihood of making such a mistake is also increasing.

This example brings to life both of the core questions addressed in this book: "How do my decisions affect the way others view me online?" and "How do those decisions affect others?" It also provides a real-life example in which you can see the various forces discussed in the following chapter at play.

CHAPTER 3

Digital is Different

"When I say, 'The Internet changes everything,'
I really mean everything."
Larry Ellison, CEO of Oracle and technology visionary

Digital is different. It's a simple idea, but fully understanding that point – internalizing it, and using it to guide your decision-making – is incredibly difficult. In fact, if students really understood this point, and could remember it every time they were online, they wouldn't run into nearly as many issues as they do. One aspect of the problem is that the lessons they have learned from the generation above them, and the inferences from the offline world that they have made while growing up, may not be relevant online. The rules have changed, but the rulebook hasn't been updated.

It's important to note that the differences between online and offline are not necessarily good or bad. They are just differences that students should be aware of so that they can anticipate the potential consequences of their actions. Understanding these points also provides us with some common ground from which we can continue the conversation. Some of these differences may seem obvious, but even the most tech-savvy students may benefit from reinforcing these concepts in their minds. In later chapters, we'll discuss how these points apply to college life and why they are so important.

DIGITAL DEVICES, DIGITAL CONTENT

The term *digital* derives from the word *digit*. It is often used to refer to electronic devices because they use computer chips that process just two digits (0's and 1's) over and over again to transmit and represent the text, pictures and videos that surround us. Living in the "digital age" refers to this first time in human existence that we are surrounded by computers. Our cars have microchips that regulate speed and help us use just the right amount of gas. Our thermostats provide a digital read-out of the temperature in our rooms. Even some toothbrushes have little microchips in them now that act as timers. Every day, all around us, we encounter digital devices. But, for the purposes of this book, I am referring specifically to the ones that help students to create content – laptops, smart-phones, video cameras, and the like.

Most of the content that you create for classes today is digital – PowerPoint presentations, Word documents, spreadsheets, online quizzes, posts to discussion forums, and more. And so is the social content that you create –

text messages, emails, tweets, Facebook updates, YouTube videos, and so on. You may be creating more digital content than you even realize – the average Facebook user posts 90 pieces of content on the site every month, and college students are far above that average.[1] In aggregate, Facebook users upload more than 30 billion items each month – and that number is continuing to grow.

Students not only create more content and communicate more frequently than ever, but the line between digital content and physical content is disappearing. Even if you are printing out your papers in order to turn them in, you probably still have a digital copy of them somewhere. And, even if you handwrite an exam, or are an art major painting on giant canvases, your content is just a simple scan or cell phone snapshot away from being stored digitally.

OPEN AUTHORSHIP

Most people can start a blog and publish their first post in under five minutes, or under 60 seconds with a bit of hustle. All you really need is an email address, and, before you know it, you've got your own space online to do whatever you want with. As blog creation website Blogger puts it, "Your blog is whatever you want it to be. There are millions of them, in all shapes and sizes, and there are no real rules." In less than a minute, you can be sharing your thoughts and opinions with the whole world.

Facebook asks "What's on your mind?" Twitter wants to know "What's happening?" A highlighted message across the top of a YouTube page suggests that you "Animate

Today's most popular websites make it very easy to create and share content

your own story or create a video slideshow. Try it now." These websites thrive on your content. In fact, without it they don't exist, and as a result they are constantly try-ing to get more of it, inviting you to update, upload, post and publish. Even sites that create their own content (from CNN.com to Vogue.com) want users to contribute, asking you to comment on their stories and share them with your friends.

User-generated content (UGC) has permeated the online world. Just six years ago, it was referred to as the "Web 2.0 revolution."[2] Today, it's just the Internet as we know it. But this is the first time in history that people have such easy access to authorship. It used to be that the news was written by trained journalists, restaurant reviews were written by professional critics, and if readers disagreed with something they had seen in a magazine, they'd be confined to their own thoughts or have to seek out a friend to discuss it with. Not anymore. Self-expression has never been easier. Update, upload, post and publish. Update, upload, post and publish. Everywhere.

In many ways, open authorship has had an incredibly positive impact on society. It has, for example, provided opportunities for talented writers and entertainers to share their works with audiences who might never have seen them otherwise. And, on a more serious note, in countries such as Iran and Egypt, political dissidents, previously repressed by their governments, have used social media to revolutionize the way that they communicate, both with one another, and with the world abroad.

On the other hand, untrained writers do not necessarily have the skills to report objectively, and many have never been forced to think about the impact that their words can have. A blogger isn't held to the same standards as a professional journalist; indeed, a blogger can essentially write whatever he or she wants with no regard for fact-checking or unbiased reporting. And yet, his or her ideas are equally accessible online – one can just as easily read the ideas of a blogger as he or she can a lead reporter in *The New York Times*. This new type of citizen journalism must be embraced with both shrewdness and caution. While it's great that you may now be exposed to more ideas, from a wider variety of sources, you must also become a more discerning consumer of online information.

Web 1.0 Called the "read-only" Web, it featured static webpages that were not frequently updated.

Web 2.0 The "read/write" Web included the rise of social networking sites, blogs, and other online communities; most important, this phase marked the introduction of user-generated content.

Web 3.0 Now the Web is becoming more personalized to the individual. Using your browsing history, physical location, and other information that you provide, online services attempt to "understand" you, and anticipate your needs. Web 3.0 is also known as the "semantic Web."

REACH AND EASE OF ACCESS

More than two billion people have access to the Internet – that's 30% of the world's population.[3] In the United States alone, there are 236 million people who could potentially access the content that you decide to publish, and even more if it gets picked up by mainstream media outlets.[4]

So, what happens when the largest collection of personalized media (such as social networking profiles, blogs, videos, and photos) meets the largest audience in the world? Internet users discover a truly open arena for finding, creating, sharing, and remixing all kinds of content.

But how do you find the content that you want to consume, and how can other people find the content that you create and share? Google was created with a mission to "organize the world's information and make it universally accessible and useful."[5] Since 1998, Google's computers have been constantly crawling the Internet, organizing and indexing webpages and the content they display, so that people can easily find the information that they need. Google, according to its official blog, has indexed over one trillion websites.[6] If students choose not to edit their privacy settings from the default "Public" on Facebook or Twitter, for example, then their parents, grandparents, professors, co-workers, and future dates can see all of this information and more with a simple Google search.

IMMEDIACY

When people press "send," their emails start traveling at almost the speed of light to their destinations. Comments, pictures, and videos that you post to a website are instantly available to every other user viewing that site. Pre-Internet, letters arrived by mail, sometimes taking weeks to reach their destinations. People wanting to publish their thoughts and dreams would at least have had to go to a copy center, make copies, and then find people to distribute their papers to. Newspaper publishers had all night to recall a story, and gossip traveled from person to person, one at a time. Now, every impulsive thought has the potential to be immediately available for all to see.

Not only is online content instantly available, but it can be created and posted from virtually anywhere. People don't need a computer anymore – smartphones (Internet-enabled phones with cameras) have made it just as easy for college students to upload photos while they're drunk at a bar, or walking back from a frat party, as it is to do while they procrastinate from doing homework in their dorm rooms. In fact, 54% of college students currently have smartphones, compared to only 27% in 2009.[7,8]

The ability to spread information used to be delayed considerably. It used to be that you had a chance to catch your breath, and give your decisions a second thought before you did any real damage. Not anymore. Not unless you really force yourself to pause and take a step back.

LACK OF CONTROL

Immediacy is a two-way street. Just as Web content can be uploaded and available in a matter of seconds, it can be downloaded just as quickly. The truth is that you don't have as much control of your content as you might think. The delete button on the websites you use – the ones that make you feel safe and in control – are still there, and usually they still work. It just may not be the case that you have the only copy of whatever you just put up. All it takes is the click of a mouse to download a picture from Facebook or a video from YouTube. With the tap of a key, users can take a snapshot of a computer screen and have their own copy of any tweet or Facebook update, AIM conversation or Skype session.

You have even less control over the content that other people post. First, this is because the original poster doesn't really have control of the content (as we just discussed). Second, this is because the laws governing online speech are still being figured out. Offline there are very clear rules – if you publish the content, you are liable for it. For example, if a newspaper prints an article that contains harmful misinformation about a person (also known as libel), then the newspaper may be sued. The newspaper is potentially liable whether it used a staff reporter or printed an opinion piece that a random reader sent in to the editor. Online, though, things get blurry. As sites have become more and more interactive, free speech has flourished. From academic debates about the future of green energy, to the more lighthearted discussions of celebrity couples, online speech has proven popular, powerful and valuable. Meanwhile, Congress has struggled to figure out a good way to keep that free speech intact, while also protecting us against the proliferation of false information.

Consider the example of reviews written on Yelp, an online service that allows users to post reviews of restaurants and shops. The owner of a restaurant may not like one of the reviews that someone posts. The review might even contain totally false allegations, and could be driving customers away from the restaurant. If that were the case, the person who wrote the review could be guilty of libel. Unfortunately, if the reviewer used a pseudonym when posting the review, or provided false identifying information when signing up, tracking down that person (subpoenas for IP addresses, etc.) so that you can get justice can be a very difficult and expensive proposition.

One might ask, "But can't the restaurant owner just sue the website?" After all, Yelp is the one continuing to make that content available, even after the owner has told Yelp that it's all a lie. Well, to date, the answer has been no. Specifically, Section 230 of the Communications Decency Act of 1996 says that "No provider or user of an interactive computer service shall be treated as the publisher or speaker of any information provided by another information content provider."[9] This means that websites can't be held liable when their users make defamatory postings. As a result, they really have no incentive to take down that content.

Ever since 1996, and even before then, there has been discussion of whether websites should be held liable for publishing defamatory content. The issue is broadly known as "intermediary liability," and has come up in Congress in various forms. There are currently discussions of requiring sites to have an "eraser button," and in Europe they are calling for the "right to be forgotten." These may be good ideas in theory, but in practice we run into another very real problem – a chilling effect on free speech.

Consider again our simple Yelp example. If a restaurant owner could get reviews removed simply by claiming that the information those reviews contain is defamatory, he could easily claim that every negative review was defamatory. As a website owner, even if you knew that a review was probably not legally defamatory, the cost of defending your position in order to not remove the content, combined with the risk that it actually is defamatory, is so high that you might very likely choose to remove every piece of content that you received a notice about. What we would be left with is an Internet full of only the nicest, most positive reviews – hence the chilling effect on free speech.

The issue is more complex, but for the purposes of this

book, suffice it to say that no such legislative action is in our near future. For now, and for the foreseeable future, when you post something online, you should acknowledge that you are giving up your control of it forever.

PERMANENCE

In many ways, permanence is the Internet's most powerful attribute. Without permanence, issues of reputation management would be much simpler. Just wait long enough, and whatever you don't like would go away. It used to be that rumors would come and go, the last one quickly forgotten as the next one spread. But with the Internet, now such rumors can be displayed online indefinitely (making the sting of cyberbullying, for example, even more painful). What we do in the digital world often lasts *forever*.

The main reason for this is that digital storage has become very inexpensive. It is so inexpensive, in fact, that companies can afford to store snapshots of webpages just in case they ever become unavailable and someone wants to see them.

One service related to this topic, but not commonly understood, is the Way Back Machine. It's available at archive.org, and run by a non-profit whose mission is "building a digital library of Internet sites and other cultural artifacts in digital form." Using the WBM, a user can see snapshots of various websites at different points in time. Wonder what Amazon looked like on October 18th, 2009? Check it out. Wonder what a friend's blog had on it three years ago? You may be able to find it on archive.org.

Consumers are also given the ability to store whatever they want, just in case they ever need it, very inexpensively, and often for free. At the moment, you can sign up for a free Gmail account, and you'll get 7.5954GB (and counting) of free Internet storage. That's enough for approximately 3,000 photos, eight hours of video, or 122,450 emails.[10] And that's free, forever. Need more? Google will sell you 20GB for just five dollars per year. 1000GB of storage costs less than a dollar per day. Don't want to pay for it? YouTube lets you upload your videos for free, and Facebook would love to host your pictures for free. The point is, storage is cheap, and every day it's getting cheaper; so there's really no reason to delete digital content. Many people use the logic that, since it is so cheap, they might as well keep everything, "just in case." College students probably have all of their emails since the day they opened their account archived away, and easily accessible through the search feature. They may even have an external hard drive filled up with pictures and videos, sitting somewhere in their rooms, holding content that they may not have looked at in years. It is increasingly true that every piece of digital content that you have ever created is sitting on a server somewhere ("in the cloud"), just in case you, or someone else, ever find that it might be useful.

Why is this important to think about? Previous generations didn't have to be as concerned as you do about mistakes following them into the future. Unless they were running for office, it was unlikely that someone would go digging through old photo albums or their personal journals to find incriminating information about them from their college years. However, with online photo sharing sites, personal blogs, and the variety of other platforms students use to share information, your past is much more easily accessible, often just a Google search away.

CHAPTER 3: KEY TAKEAWAYS

– We are surrounded by computers and smartphones, providing constant connectivity to the Web, and allowing for the easy creation of incredibly large amounts digital content.

– Today, everyone is a content creator, and what each of us produces can quickly reach an audience of millions.

– As soon as your digital content is posted online, you are no longer in control of where it goes, who sees it, or how long it stays online.

– Digital content often stays online forever.

CHAPTER 4

A Library, YouTube, and Death Threats

"I lost my temper on stage. I was at a comedy club
trying to do my act and I got heckled and I took it badly and went
into a rage and said some pretty nasty things…"
Michael Richards (Kramer on *Seinfeld*) on *The Letterman Show*
apologizing after a racist tirade

It was finals week. She was stressed – and annoyed. She needed to vent. YouTube seemed like an obvious choice. It would be really easy to share with her friends, so they could all agree and sympathize with her. It was so easy that she hardly had to think about it. Click. Click. Talk. Click. Click. And it was done – uploaded and ready to be shared.

Nicole Banks (name changed), a UCLA Junior majoring in Political Science uploaded a webcam video to YouTube. She titled it "Asians in the Library."[11] It was a three-minute-long video of her, seated at her desk, ranting into the camera about how much Asians in the library were annoying her that week, and in general. The video is offensive from the beginning and gets progressively worse. You can find the video on YouTube simply by searching for "UCLA Asian rant," but here are some highlights, or perhaps more accurately, lowlights:

> So we know that I'm not the most politically correct person, so don't take this offensively. I don't mean it towards any of my friends. I mean it towards random people that I don't even know in the library.
> …
> The problem is… these hordes of Asian people that UCLA accepts into our school every single year… which is fine, but if you're gonna come to UCLA then use American manners!
> …
> Hi, in America, we do not talk on our cell phones in the library! I swear, every five minutes I will be, ok not five minutes, say like, fifteen minutes, I'll be like deep into my studying, into my political science theories and arguments and all that stuff, getting it all down, like typing away furiously, blah blah blah, and then all of a sudden when I'm about to like reach an epiphany, over here from somewhere "Ohhhhhhh, ching chong, ling long, ting tong, ohhhhhhh." Are you freaking kidding me? In the middle of finals week?
> …
> I swear it's like they're going through their whole family, just checking on everybody from the tsunami thing – I mean, I know okay, that sounds horrible, like I feel bad for all the people affected by the tsunami, but if you're gonna go call your address book, like you might as well go outside because if something is wrong you might really freak out….

Her friends watched the video and quickly decided it was worth sharing. And shared it was. The link was originally posted on Facebook; then it spread quickly through UCLA and onto other college campuses. Within two days, the video had gone viral, and hundreds of thousands of people had watched Nicole's exasperated rant. Nicole realized that she had made a big mistake, and she took down the video; but, unfortunately, it was too late. The video had already been downloaded and reposted through other accounts, and on other sites. She couldn't take it back – it was out of her control. The video continued to spread. It was featured on countless blogs, and even made its way onto TV.[12,13] Today, on YouTube alone, reposts of the video have been viewed more than 10,000,000 times. Combine that with the responses and parodies, and there have been more than 27,000,000 views.

The UCLA Chancellor responded to the growing controversy by saying, "I am appalled by the thoughtless and hurtful comments of a UCLA student posted on YouTube…. Like many of you, I recoil when someone invokes the right of free expression to demean other individuals or groups."[14] Meanwhile, students on campus were making their sentiments known as well. The creator of the video was ostracized and began receiving death threats.

She never imagined that this would happen. She even claims that she was just trying to be funny. She apologized by issuing the following statement to the campus newspaper:

> In an attempt to produce a humorous YouTube video, I have offended the UCLA community and the entire

Reposts of the original video "Asians in the Library," along with parodies and responses, have received more than 27 million views on YouTube

Asian culture. I am truly sorry for the hurtful words I said and the pain it caused to anyone who watched the video. Especially in the wake of the ongoing disaster in Japan, I would do anything to take back my insensitive words. I could write apology letters all day and night, but I know they wouldn't erase the video from your memory, nor would they act to reverse my inappropriate action.

In that same letter, she goes on to say:

I made a mistake. My mistake, however, has led to the harassment of my family, the publishing of my personal information, death threats, and being ostracized from an entire community. Accordingly, for personal safety reasons, I have chosen to no longer attend classes at UCLA.[15]

Nicole wasn't thinking about who might see her video, or how they might perceive it. To be sure, she didn't anticipate that millions of people would watch her video and feel disturbed, offended, and hurt by what she was saying. She thought it was funny (lol) and then realized it wasn't (OMG!) – and it has turned out to be a mistake that has changed the course of her life forever. For us, it further highlights the importance of thinking carefully about the content that you share online.

CHAPTER 5

Your Life, Online

"Oh great, so now there's nothing they don't know
about me and my private life."
Rihanna, on the spread of personal pictures and information online

Students create an enormous amount of digital content
every day and in a variety of ways. For their classes, they
are typing papers, creating presentations, shooting videos, completing online exams, and contributing to discussion forums, just to name a few. Outside the classroom
they are creating even more digital content – emails and
texts to friends and family, Facebook updates, Foursquare
check-ins, tweets, videos, blogs, and more. In fact, the former
CEO of Google, Eric Schmidt, has asserted that, every
two days, people are now creating as much information as
was created, in total, between the beginning of time and
2003.[16] As heavy users of social media with nearly constant
Internet access, college students are among the most significant contributors to that massive amount of information.

CARELESS CONTENT CREATION

The content that students create can essentially be separated into two buckets – academic and social, and there are two big differences between these types. First, no one is grading the social content; and, as any college professor can tell you, when it's not being graded, it doesn't typically get a whole lot of thought or effort. Second, no one is making money from the academic content that students are creating – professors aren't paid by the essay, or for each completed math problem.

Companies, on the other hand, do make money on your social content; so they have made it very easy to create that content. These companies want using their services to be as easy and natural as breathing – something you do every day without even thinking about it. Take a picture on your cell phone at a party and you can upload it to Facebook in a matter of seconds. Stop into a restaurant and all it takes is a couple of taps on your cell phone to check in. It takes five mouse clicks to upload a video to YouTube and only three to publish a new post on your blog. These companies aren't evil – they don't want people to put up content that is embarrassing or bad for them – they just want lots of content, because that's how they make money. Combine both of these factors and what you get from students is a very casual sort of content creation, and, more often than not, casual gives way to careless.

I don't mean careless in the completely thoughtless sort of way. In fact, some sorts of social content get a lot of thought before they are created. One college student I interviewed noted, "Well, I only upload the photos I look good in." Another student commented, "It's not like I tweet everything I do. I just tweet the interesting stuff."

The Facebook Blues: Students are often presented with a biased view of their friends' lives on social media sites – a view that shows only the best of times. As a result, students can sometimes feel depressed or unpopular, as if they aren't having as much fun as everyone else. Remember, though, that most people don't post updates about brushing their teeth, or pictures of themselves crying in their room or reading in the library. Instead, they post pictures of the fun parties they go to, and the great meals out with friends. But, just like you, your friends are also staying in some nights to study, cleaning their rooms, dealing with boyfriend or girlfriend drama, and so on.

Unfortunately, this is a rather superficial set of criteria upon which decisions are made. So, when I say careless, I really mean without regard to all those ways we discussed in Chapter 3 that the digital world works differently, and without regard to the long-term impact that the content might have on one's reputation. While there are many explanations for this carelessness (doing things in a rush, genuinely innocuous content, etc.), there are some more subtle explanations worth exploring.

SUPERIORITY BIAS

There are two significant psychological explanations for this carelessness. The first is called Superiority Bias. Research has found that Superiority Bias is incredibly common, even among highly educated, self-aware people.[17] The basic premise is that people generally consider them-selves to have more desirable qualities, and fewer undesirable qualities, than the average person. This can't be true, of course, because not everyone can be better than average. Someone is wrong. In fact, statistically, most people are wrong – even the ones that really are above average aren't typically as high above average as they think.

As a result of this bias, it becomes very easy for students to dismiss examples like that of the Duke Sex List and the UCLA Asian Rant, because students tell themselves that they are smarter, or more forward-thinking, than the students in those examples, and that they would never do something like that themselves. I would argue that anyone could have made those same mistakes. Both women attended top universities – ostensibly, these were "smart" women. Gossip about sex is commonplace on college campuses, and frustrations resulting from cultural differ-ences (and the eventual learnings that arise from those frustrations) are common as well. While most such events don't get nearly so much media coverage, there is nothing else so extraordinary about either situation that should lead you to believe that you could not make a similar mistake.

AMBIGUITY EFFECT AND ATTRIBUTE SUBSTITUTION

The second explanation for careless content is the result of two combined phenomena called Ambiguity Effect and Attribute Substitution. Ambiguity Effect refers to the natural human inclination to avoid scenarios with lots of missing or unclear information, or scenarios in which the probability of something occurring is unknown.[18] We are presented with exactly such scenarios every day online. How many people will see what I'm posting? Who will see it? What will they think? Will it ever be on the first page of my Google results? None of these questions has a definite answer; so our tendency is not to ask them – instead, our tendency is to avoid them.

Attribute Substitution explains the particular manner in which we avoid those questions. Attribute Substitution refers to peoples' tendencies to make difficult, complex judgments easier by subconsciously substituting them for simpler problems.[19] In the case of college students creating online content, this typically means students telling themselves that only their friends will see their content. They have a much clearer idea of how their friends will react, and have thus avoided the more difficult problem of who else might see the content, and whether it might ever be a problem for them in the future.

For all of these reasons, students convince themselves that everything that they are sharing is fine. But, as we saw with the Duke Sex List and the UCLA Asian Rant, it's not always fine. The content you create now can have serious implications later.

YOU ARE CREATING YOUR REPUTATION

Collectively, all of the digital content that you and others create becomes your online reputation. And today, that's the reputation that matters most. People have already looked you up online, and that is going to continue to happen for the rest of your life. Before you were admitted to school, the admissions office may have done a quick Google or Facebook search of your name. Your roommate probably searched for information about you before move-in. Your parents may have searched your name to check in on you. A curious professor may have searched all of his students' names to get a better sense of who would be in her upcoming class. After you graduate, future employers, friends and dates will also Google you. And you have probably Googled your friends, family, classmates and professors.

All of this searching is not surprising – it's the easiest way to get information about someone. Are you trustworthy? Wealthy? Smart? A trouble-maker? A drunk? A jerk? In an ideal world, people would have to get to know you and decide all of these things for themselves. After all, not everything on the Internet is true. But the reality is that no one has time for that. Most people don't get past the first half of the first page of search results (making those headlines all the more important).[20] Google, for better or worse, provides an easy shortcut, and has become the first place that people look for information about someone.

The trouble with all this Googling is that not everything online is accurate, and, even if it is, it doesn't tell the full story. Your online reputation may not really reflect who you are. As we discussed in Chapter 3, the Internet is a wide-open canvas, upon which pretty much anyone can write pretty much anything. There is no mega-computer checking to see whether the image that you, or that others portray of you, is correct. No one is actively pulling

The days of "What happens in Vegas, stays in Vegas" are long gone

down false content or verifying true content on your behalf.

People will judge you based on what they find online. Just as students have cognitive biases that affect their decisions of what to share or not share online, so too do the people who are searching for information about those students. Understanding your audience's biases is a critical part of making informed decisions regarding the content that you decide to post.

OVERESTIMATING THE INTERNET'S VALIDITY

The Internet has certain inherent characteristics that tend to make it seem like information you find on it is more trustworthy than it actually is. Consider how incorrect information was spread pre-Internet. False facts were typically spoken – embodied by the common joke that "83% of statistics are made up on the spot." Defamatory comments and gossip were typically spoken as well, or written on bathroom walls. Meanwhile, newspapers were held to a very high standard in what they would report, and printed corrections if anything that they had published proved to be incorrect. Encyclopedias were seen as gold standards of truth and accuracy. So, when the transition to finding information on the Internet happened, our sense of the trustworthiness of sources got mixed up. Internet content is text and image-based, not spoken, and we access it from our computers, which seem so reliable (unlike bathroom stalls). As a result, people question the accuracy of Internet content far less than they should.

FIRST IMPRESSION BIAS

In addition to giving Internet content more credibility than they should, people also often weigh that information more heavily than they should. Two common psychological biases related to the weighting of information are: First Impression Bias, and Negative Information Bias.

First Impression Bias is exactly as one would expect – people weigh the information that they receive first about a person more heavily than what they hear after. Malcolm Gladwell's well-known book *Blink* offers an in-depth look at some of the benefits, and often detriments, of our quick judgments. In it, he asserts that, "Snap judgments are, first of all, enormously quick: they rely on the thinnest slices of experience ... they are also unconscious."[21]

Remember Caitlin Upton, Miss Teen South Carolina 2007? If you do, you probably remember her based on her response to the following prompt: "Recent polls have shown 1/5 of Americans can't locate the U.S. on a world map. Why do you think this is?" She responded:

> I personally believe that U.S. Americans are unable to do so because, some... people out there in our nation don't have maps and, I believe that our education like, such as, in South Africa and, the Iraq, everywhere like such as, and, I believe that they should, our education over here in the U.S. should help the U.S., or, should help South Africa and should help the Iraq and the Asian countries, so we will be able to build up our future, for our children.[22]

Her nonsensical response has since earned her more than 60,000,000 YouTube views and an appearance on *The Today Show*. And now that's all we remember about her. For most Americans, it was our first impression of her. So, what would it take to convince you that she was a good student? Your first impression of her was that she isn't very bright; so when you hear that her high school principal said, "She took college-prep and honors courses and performed well,"[23] you might not really believe it. Instead, you think he's just being nice because he feels bad for her. But the truth is, all you know is that an 18-year-old on stage, with millions of people watching at home, flubbed a question. As Caitlin put it, "Everybody makes mistakes. I'm human."[24]

First impressions matter, and regardless of whether your audience is right or wrong in its assessment of you, the phenomenon is real and very relevant. Your online reputation is often the first impression that you create. Before someone knows anything about you, you have a clean slate. Then, he or she searches your name online and begins to form an impression of you. For example, did you search your freshman-year roommate's name online before you moved in? It's a safe bet that he or she searched yours, and what that person found made a first impression. This impression could be good or bad – you seem very caring, very smart, or very immature. Whatever the impression, any contradictory information received after the original impression is made comes under suspicion and must be proven – you must fight to refute the impression that has already begun to form in his or her mind. You're much better off giving a strong first impression if you can.

NEGATIVE INFORMATION BIAS

The second notable bias that people searching for you online may have is Negative Information Bias. This phenomenon occurs when people weigh negative information more heavily than other information.[25] Online, this bias can compound the effects of a bad first impression. The basic logic of it is that "bad" people do "good" things, but "good" people don't do "bad" things; so information about people doing bad things is more telling about someone's character. Here's an example: what do you know about Richard Nixon? Most people's answers include the words

Superiority Bias: Most people consider themselves to have more desirable qualities, and fewer undesirable qualities, than the average person, even though this is statistically impossible. For example, people generally believe they are less likely than others to make mistakes online.

Ambiguity Effect: People tend to avoid questions that do not have a clear, definite answer. This is part of why they post things online without first considering how other people might perceive them, or what would happen if those things resurface years later.

Attribute Substitution: People generally replace complex questions, like what the world might think of the content they post online, with simpler ones, such as how their close friends will react.

First Impression Bias: Information we receive first about a person tends to stick in our minds more than the things we learn later about them. We make unconscious "snap judgments" based on first impressions and it's hard to change our minds later.

Negative Information Bias: People tend to weigh negative information more heavily than positive or neutral information. This means it is easier for them to remember the negative news stories of the day, or a person's mistakes and immoral deeds.

"impeached," "Watergate," maybe "crook," and not much else. The idea that he could be a "good" person is harder for people to conjure up because of the variety of negative associations they have from his past transgressions. His years of service in Congress, along with the new anticrime laws he implemented, his efforts to improve relations with communist China, his victory in ending the draft, and his oversight of the first moon landing, are all thrown out the window. People focus on negative information and fail to see the positives as a result.

PERCEPTION IS REALITY

Finally, and perhaps most important, you have to remember that for many people who will Google you, you are starting from a blank slate. These people don't necessarily have the context that you might hope for them to have when they are reading about you online. Consider the example of a gay classmate posting something such as, "This Lady Gaga album is sooooo gay." The people who know him may understand that he means that quite literally – perhaps Lady Gaga is singing very pro-gay lyrics; but to anyone who reads that and doesn't know him, he might seem like just an ignorant college kid using "gay" as a slur. You don't have to be homophobic to be perceived as homophobic. And you don't have to be racist, irresponsible, a drunkard, etc., to be perceived in those ways either.

REAL CONSEQUENCES

Let's recap this chapter so far. You are creating your online reputation, possibly more carelessly than you should. People are searching for you online, and what they find is having a real and significant impact on the way they perceive you. Now, we take a quick look at the way that this could actually impact your life.

We've considered several examples that have made

national headlines, and there are many more that we haven't covered but could have. There was a scandal at USC about a misogynistic email allegedly sent out by one of its fraternities; there was a football player in Texas who was kicked off the team after posting a racist Facebook update, and so on. But, chances are, you aren't going to be one of these cases. It is unlikely that you will be the next national college social media disaster. However, that doesn't mean that there won't be consequences from your digital content. In fact, I can guarantee that your online reputation will have an impact on your life – that impact just may not be quite so obvious as a national scandal.

GETTING THE JOB

By far, the most common area where poor decisions in social media are having negative consequences is in employment. This is particularly hard for students to understand because many have not had serious jobs before going to college. A summer internship during college is, for many students, the first time that they have worked in a corporate setting. For most, the hiring process their senior year is the first time that they will go through a rigorous interview process. Without ever having had full-time jobs, and certainly without having been in the position of having to hire someone themselves, many college students struggle with the idea that employers really care about this stuff. I have even heard students make comments such as, "Well if [Company X] is doing that, then it isn't the type of place I want to work anyhow." The problem

with that attitude is that it limits your options pretty substantially. It also may not be the case that you will feel the
same way in a few years.

Today, 70% of recruiters admit to having rejected a
candidate based on information that they have found
online,[26] and the actual number may be even higher. The
three most common reasons for not hiring someone were,
"concerns about the candidate's lifestyle," "inappropriate
comments and text written by the candidate," and "unsuit-
able photos, videos and information." What "inappropriate" means in this context is somewhat vague, but another
survey found that "content about drinking or using drugs,"
"poor communication skills" and "discriminatory comments," were among recruiters' top concerns with regard
to online content.[27] Think about all of the content that you
have up online right now. Does any of that content fall into
any of those categories? For many college students, it does.

The content that you put up online isn't likely to get you
the job, but it very well may prevent it – careless content
creation can come back to bite you. Companies don't go
online looking for the awards you forgot to tell them about.
They are looking for red flags – things that you are smart
enough not to say in an interview, but might be willing to
have said online. *The New York Times* reported about one
student who listed "smokin' blunts" as an interest, and another who had posted public photos of herself passed out
drunk.[28] Needless to say, neither got the jobs he and she
were seeking. One recruiter commented, "A lot of it makes
me think, what kind of judgment does this person have?
Why are you allowing this to be viewed publicly, effectively,

or semipublicly?"

Had the *The New York Times* article not been written, the students may never have known the reasons for which they had been denied employment. Companies don't have to tell you why they decided not to interview or hire you. You don't get a chance to explain why you were giving the finger to the camera man, or that the line of white powder in your picture was just flour because it was a rock star theme party. They just don't call. If you haven't searched your name on Google in a while, there might be something negative or offensive that you're not even aware of. And who knows how many opportunities you've already missed out on as a result.

SOCIAL BACKGROUND CHECKS

New services are also making it easier for companies to do this kind of online social research. Recently, a company named Social Intelligence has gotten quite a bit of press because the Federal Trade Commission (FTC) completed an investigation of it and confirmed that everything that it was doing was legal. In essence, employers hire Social Intelligence to perform background checks. If you want a job at a company that uses Social Intelligence, you have to agree to the social background check. Social Intelligence then goes into stalker mode, with skills that would put your super-smart, computer-science friends to shame. Social Intelligence employees scour the Internet – blogs, public databases, Facebook, Twitter, Flickr, Craigslist, etc., to find out whatever they can about you.

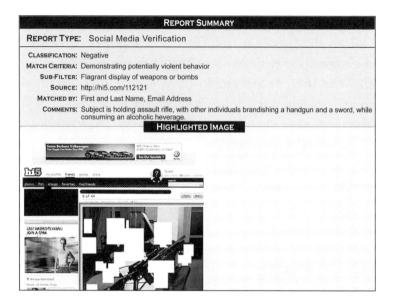

REPORT SUMMARY	
REPORT TYPE:	Social Media Verification
CLASSIFICATION:	Negative
MATCH CRITERIA:	Demonstrating potentially violent behavior
SUB-FILTER:	Flagrant display of weapons or bombs
SOURCE:	http://hi5.com/112121
MATCHED BY:	First and Last Name, Email Address
COMMENTS:	Subject is holding assault rifle, with other individuals brandishing a handgun and a sword, while consuming an alcoholic heverage.

HIGHLIGHTED IMAGE

REPORT SUMMARY	
REPORT TYPE:	Social Media Verification
CLASSIFICATION:	Negative
MATCH CRITERIA:	Racism or other Discriminatory Tendencies
SUB-FILTER:	Other obvious racist leaning or proclivities
SOURCE:	http://www.facebook.com
MATCHED BY:	First/last name, city,state, email.
COMMENTS:	He "likes" on his facebook a discriminatory group.

HIGHLIGHTED IMAGE

Two examples of reports created by Social Intelligence

It's worth noting that they are only using the information that you have provided your potential employer – primarily the name, address, email address and phone number on your resume. These four pieces of information allow them to triangulate on all sorts of other information about you. Have you ever posted your email address in the comment section of a blog? Now they've got your username for that site. How about your phone number in a Craigslist post? Now that anonymous Craigslist post isn't so anonymous.

If they find something controversial (in accordance with legal guidelines), a report is sent to the employer, and that's probably the end of the interview process for you. One example of a "negative finding" shows that a student had "liked" a Facebook page called, "I shouldn't have to press 1 for English. We are in the United States. Learn the language." (And, no, it wasn't the same student who posted the UCLA Asian Rant). There are thousands of students who liked that same page. The student probably thought that it was funny (lol). Then his potential employer received a report that said "Match Criteria: Racism or Other Discriminatory Tendencies." Unfortunately for the student, there were enough other candidates who didn't have any negative search results, and he didn't get the job (OMG!).

This is the future of the employment process. Employment is an expensive proposition for companies. A mistake costs them a lot of money, so they want to use all of the information that they are (legally) able to. This is no longer a trend. The social background check is here to stay.

BEYOND EMPLOYMENT

While employment should be a major concern, it shouldn't be the only one – it's not just employers searching the Web for information about you. Several colleges and universities have admitted to using Internet searches to screen candidates, for both undergraduate and graduate-school admissions decisions.[29] Not going to school ever again? Don't care about getting a job? You probably still care about getting a date. In a recent survey of more than 1,000 singles in their early twenties,[30] 81% said that they do a search for their date on Google or Facebook before meeting. A good first impression online can make the date go a whole lot better, and a bad one can prevent it from going at all. And there are countless other people out there that might do a search of your name online, each with a different potential consequence – be it the conservative grandmother who writes you out of the will, or the future landlady who doesn't think that you look like her kind of tenant.

The important thing to realize is that whatever someone finds out about you, whether good or bad, true or false, it will impact the way that you are assessed; so, managing your online reputation – being a conscious, rather than careless, creator of content online – is critically important in nearly all facets of your life.

CHAPTER 5: KEY TAKEAWAYS

— Students create massive amounts of content, often putting little consideration into who might see it and how it might be perceived.

— There are many psychological reasons for careless content creation, including Superiority Bias, Ambiguity Effect, and Attribute Substitution.

— Collectively, all of the digital content that you and others create becomes your online reputation.

— Your audience is biased and puts disproportionately more weight on the first and any negative information that they find about you.

— 70% of recruiters admit to rejecting a candidate based on information that they have found online.

— Your online reputation will have a significant impact on your life in a variety of contexts, including dating, grad-school admissions, and employment opportunities.

CHAPTER 6

Becoming a Conscious Creator of Content

"Little girls think it's necessary to put all their business on... Facebook, and I think it's a shame... I'm all about mystery."
Stevie Nicks, lead singer of Fleetwood Mac

There is a thin line between creative and creepy, funny and offensive, personal and private. The past several chapters have helped you understand the potential impact of your digital content. This chapter explores the content of your content – helping you think about where you want to draw your own lines with regard to what you share online. In this chapter, we remain focused on the personal consequences of your decisions, saving our consideration of how those decisions may affect others for Chapters 9 and 10. However, it is worth noting that to truly become a conscious creator of content, you must consider not only the personal consequences of your digital decisions, but also their effect on others.

The key to avoiding negative consequences associated

with the digital content you create is to make deliberate decisions – understanding the full range of places where content may end up, all of the people who might see it, and the variety of ways in which they might react. Thinking thoroughly through those steps every time you post an update, share an article, or upload a picture would be unreasonably time-consuming and unrealistic. Instead, it makes sense to take some time in advance to think about the types of content you will and will not share online and understand why.

WHY ARE YOU DOING THIS?

The question of "Why?" preempts any other questions that you might ask yourself. Why do you have a Twitter account in the first place? Why are you posting pictures on Facebook? What are you hoping to get out of having a blog? Ultimately, why are you using social media the way you are? There are many perfectly legitimate answers to these questions, while you may find that other answers you arrive at aren't very substantial.

Social media is a great pastime, and for some that answer may be enough; however, there are also some superficial answers that you should challenge yourself to examine more closely. For example, you might answer that you post pictures to Facebook because you like sharing with your friends. But why? If you consider the question further, you might say that it's an easy way to get pictures to the other people who were at the same event, and they appreciate having them so that they may share in the memories. An alternate answer might be that you like posting pictures because you want people who weren't there to see how much fun you were having. Both are real reasons that people post pictures on Facebook, but each implies a need for a very different audience.

Perhaps you are writing a political blog. If your goal is to show your support for a particular party or issue about which you are passionate, you might not mind making more controversial statements. On the other hand, if your only real goal is to practice your writing and you just happened to choose politics as a topic, you might want to take a more moderate stance so as to avoid any potential future conflict.

In the process of answering this fundamental question, you may also realize that you don't have a good reason for certain types of content creation. Maybe Twitter isn't actually adding that much value to your life. Or it may be that leaving comments on celebrity gossip sites isn't how you want to spend your time.

The power of suggestion can be very strong, but you should remind yourself that just because these sites are asking you to contribute doesn't mean that you have to. Knowing why you are creating the content in the first place allows you to weigh that value against the potential risks.

IS NOW THE RIGHT TIME?

Timing, as they say, is everything, and that certainly applies to social media. This is not a question of whether something should ever be posted (we'll get to that), just whether there is a difference between doing it now and doing it later. The problem generally manifests itself in terms of either real-time location information or temporary judgment impairment.

Giving information about your location (via Twitter posts, Foursquare check-ins, etc.) may be done while you are at a certain place, or afterwards. If you are trying to let a bunch of your friends know where you are so that you can all meet up, real-time updates may make sense. On the other hand, if you are just trying to keep a record of where you have been, you can always do that when you get home. There might be reasons why you would not want to broadcast your location to everyone you know, and especially to people whom you don't know. While there have been very few cases, there is a risk that opportunists will use the information of where you are against you.

The other issue related to timing has to do with temporary judgment impairment. This section's subtitle almost could have been, "Are you drunk?" If the answer is yes, it's better to stay offline until you sober up. Drunken content creation is even worse than careless content creation, because your judgment is so severely impaired.

The term "drunk dialing" is common, and, as more communication happens through Facebook, and other social media, new terms are popping up. Urban Dictionary offers the following tongue-in-cheek definition of "drunk Facebooking":

> See drunk dialing, but refers primarily to using Facebook-
> .com or other social networking sites (like MySpace.com)

to send your inebriated and often absurd messages. Generally only used if drunk dialing is not an option (i.e., the person you are drunk Facebooking would not willingly give you their [sic] cell phone number).

Even your text messages can end up online. TextsFromLastNight.com is a site that encourages people to send in text messages they've sent or received while drunk, so that they can be displayed for the world to see (and laugh at). They choose to display only the area codes associated with each text, but imagine if they, or someone else, decided to post text messages with real names or phone numbers next to them. Suddenly, much less funny.

Alcohol isn't the only way that your judgment might be temporarily impaired – high emotions can cause you to make poor digital decisions. If you are sad, depressed, angry, or overwhelmed, think carefully before taking to your social media profiles. People say things they don't mean when they are upset – often things they would not want everyone they know to hear. And if you say it online, it becomes harder to take it back. Furthermore, involving a satellite of Facebook "friends" and Twitter followers in your personal life may or may not be to your advantage. When it comes to emotional events, consider talking to your real friends in person or on the phone, in a one-on-one or small-group environment.

The final question to consider with regard to the timing of your content creation is: am I especially likely to be scrutinized right now? If you are an athlete, you are always subject to increased attention, and even more so during your on-season. If you just got elected president of your sorority, or to the Senate of your student government, you may have more people paying attention to your digital media presence, sometimes even actively looking for ways to discredit you. And, of course, if you are in the middle of looking for an internship, or a full-time job, you should know that your employer is Googling you. There is never a good time to let your guard down online, and during certain times, it is worth being extra cautious.

WHERE IS YOUR LINE BETWEEN PUBLIC AND PRIVATE?

There has certainly been a trend over the past several years toward living our lives very publicly online – inane tweets about brushing one's teeth, and provocative blog posts recounting details of a blind date. There are some people who would be perfectly happy to have every moment of their lives videotaped and put up on YouTube for the whole world to see. Nonetheless, most people still prefer a bit more privacy and discretion. Even if you don't have any particular political aspirations, or ever expect to be famous, it doesn't mean that you don't want to keep some thoughts, some photos, some information to yourself and your close friends or family.

Most social media services allow you to choose from a variety of privacy levels, and utilizing those options can be very valuable. For services like Facebook and Google+, where you can choose specific groups of people to see specific types of content, at the very least you should separate your contacts into three groups – friends and family (people you know and trust), professional (people you work with and want to stay connected to, but who don't need to know about your personal life), and acquaintances (people you don't actually know very well at all, but still accept their friendship requests). Some people further separate these groups, for example, splitting friends and family, and then splitting friends into high school friends and college friends.

For each of these groups, it is important to identify what you are sharing with them and why. Do you want to share your medical information online? Are you the type to kiss and tell? What information do you want publicly available to everyone and what information do only your friends need?

Remember, though, that with any digital media, even if you think it's private, it's only a few clicks away from being public. Remember that the author of the Duke Sex List sent her PowerPoint to just three of her friends – people whom, presumably, she trusted very much. As soon as you share your content with others, there is a possibility they will share it with others as well. So, if you are going to share your content, you need to weigh the benefit of sharing it with friends against the likelihood that it will also be shared with others, and what the implications of that might be. Sometimes, in the digital age, your only real choice is between sharing your content with everyone and sharing your content with no one.

HOW CONTROVERSIAL DO YOU WANT TO BE?

Have you heard any good jokes lately? Have you heard any that you and your friends would find funny, but others might find offensive? I'm sure you can think of a joke like this. It's the kind of joke that you wouldn't tell to a stranger – it's too risky, having a high probability of awkwardness and far too much potential to offend. If you were to tell the joke at all, you would probably want to save it for a small group of friends who you know will find it funny. And, while that may seem intuitive offline, something seems to get lost in the online translation – jokes such as those are shared every day on Facebook and Twitter.

When sharing information online, keep this in mind: people differ. It's such a simple concept that it is easy to gloss over; so it bears repeating...people differ. College campuses especially are a place of rich diversity, bringing together students from all over the world with different genders, races, religions, sexual orientations, wealth levels, work experiences, etc. While you may find a particular picture, comment or article funny, someone else might find it deeply offensive. Considering the range of reactions people can have is a key component of being a thoughtful social media user. Knowing that, when you post something, you are not only posting it for like-minded people to see, but for a variety of people whose backgrounds you may know only in a cursory way, is an important part of making responsible decisions online.

That is also how life outside of college is, except with the added component of age diversity, which brings with

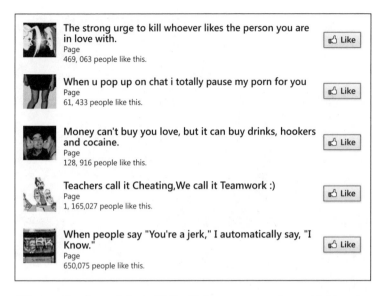

Thousands of people have "Liked" these pages, perhaps thinking that they are funny, but many people would disagree

it an even broader range of experiences. As a result of all this diversity, not everyone sees the world in the same way. Something you find completely mundane, someone else may find decidedly inflammatory. When you create digital content, considering how others might view that content is a critical step before deciding whether to share it.

Miley Cyrus learned this lesson the hard way when a picture of her pulling back the sides of her eyes – a gesture sometimes, unfortunately, used to mock Asian people, found its way online. It looks as though she and all of her friends were having fun – not intending to be hurtful. When Miley apologized, she said, "I've also been told there are some people upset about some pictures taken of me

Miley Cyrus and friends making "goofy faces"

with friends making goofy faces! Well, I'm sorry if those
people looked at those pics and took them wrong and out
of context!... In no way was I making fun of any ethnicity! I
was simply making a goofy face." Asian fans and advocacy
groups, however, disagreed, and for weeks she dealt with
being called a racist in the press.

It was a case of differing worldviews and sensibilities. It
clearly had never occurred to Miley that the face she was
making might be offensive. And even though she may believe
in her heart that she is not racist, perceptions matter, and
Miley had to deal with the consequences.

Imagine, for a moment, how a similar scenario might
play out on your campus. Perhaps there has been a fra-

ternity party with a theme that a particular group has found to be offensive. Perhaps a writer for the campus newspaper wrote an article that unintentionally triggered a campus-wide debate. Whatever the case may be, you can rest assured that it happens on college campuses all the time. Failing to think about how others will perceive your actions, regardless of your intentions, is a trap to which everyone can fall prey.

Content can be controversial in a host of different ways. Racism, sexism, homophobia, references to drug and alcohol use, and vulgarity all run rampant online. The average college student participates in some, if not all, of these behaviors at least at some point in his or her college career. Becoming aware of how online content may be perceived by others is a prerequisite to managing your online reputation.

An equally controversial category, deserving recognition all on its own, is sexual content. While there are many different ways that a student might create sexual content (a 42-page PowerPoint, for example), by far the most common way is the sext – a sexual text message. Most sexts involve texting flirtatious, and more often graphically exual, language back and forth. Screenshots of cell phone text message windows make those conversations easy to share, and that ease of sharing can lead to trouble. More troublesome, though, are the pictures that get sent from phone to phone.

The most important rule to know about taking sexual photos is that under absolutely no circumstances should you take sexual photos of anyone under 18 years old, including yourself. Such photos are considered child pornography by U.S. law, and creating, soliciting, or sharing those photos can have very serious legal consequences. Any such action is criminal. Don't do it. Ever.

Now, assuming that you are over 18, you have a choice to make. Do you want to take nude or even semi-nude pictures of yourself? If so, why? Often, the reason is that a boyfriend or girlfriend is pressuring you to do so; but, if you don't want to do it, just don't. Many students, when they are able to step back and objectively reflect on the situation, decide that the benefits of these pictures are outweighed by the risks.

You may think that you are sending these pictures to just one person, and you may really trust that person, perhaps even love him or her; but, you should anticipate that those pictures will be shared. First of all, it can be incredibly tempting to show off a hot picture to one's friends. Also, it can happen accidentally, while a friend is flipping through the photos on another friend's phone. And what happens if the phone is lost or stolen? Your photos could end up anywhere.

If you are in a relationship this may be the last thing that you want to hear, but you should also remember that most college relationships don't last. It may feel as though everything is great and you two will be together forever, but people and situations can change very quickly in college, and that can sometimes mean the unanticipated end of a relationship. What happens if he or she becomes your ex? If the relationship ends badly, where might your pictures wind up? If you think you might regret having taken the pictures if you break up, then it's probably best not to take them in the first place.

YOUR LIFE, YOUR DECISIONS

When you meet and interact with people in the real world, it is likely that you consider how you will come off: what you are going to say, how you are going to represent yourself, what types of things you share with them. If you don't already, you should consider bringing this same type of discretion to the information that you share online. No one can tell you the answers to these questions. Everyone has a different situation, each requiring unique guidelines regarding digital content creation. It is critical, however, that you have thought through these questions and that you have come up with answers, fully understanding the risks that you may be taking along with the potential benefits.

CHAPTER 6: KEY TAKEAWAYS

— The best way to create a positive online reputation is to think carefully about all of the content that you share on the Web.

— It is impossible to stop and do the rigorous thinking necessary to protect yourself every time that you post something online.

— Knowing the answers ahead of time to these four key questions will help you make better decisions: Why are you doing this? Is now the right time? Where is your line between public and private? How controversial do you want to be?

CHAPTER 7

Active Reputation Management

"Reputation, reputation, reputation! Oh, I have lost
my reputation! I have lost the immortal part of myself..."
Cassio, in William Shakespeare's *Othello*

Once you have decided where your lines are – what you are comfortable sharing, and with whom – you can worry less about future mistakes you may make and start actively managing the content that you have already created. This chapter gives concrete advice on things you can do today, and strategies that you can employ in the long-term, to keep your online reputation intact.

SEVEN STEPS THAT YOU CAN TAKE RIGHT NOW

By now, hopefully it is clear just how important managing your online presence truly is. It's so easy to put off these simple steps to do at some point in the future, but you should challenge yourself to do them right now, between reading each of these steps. Then, tackle the longer, harder stuff described at the end of the chapter, tomorrow, and in small chunks every day thereafter.

1. Google Yourself

It's amazing how many people haven't done this. And, of those who have, it's amazing how few have done it recently. This is something you have to do at least once every three months.

First, you must turn off Google's customized search results feature. On their Help page, Google explains that they customize search results based on your "past search activity on Google, such as searches you've done or results you've clicked." Usually this is a good thing, yielding results that are more likely to be relevant to you, but, for our purposes, it will need to be turned off so you can view your results in the same way that others are likely to see them. The easiest way to do this is to sign out of your Google account (if applicable) and delete your cookies. There are other ways to do this that will allow you to preserve your cookies, which you can easily find by searching for "turn off customized search."

Now, with the custom search featured turned off, type your name into the Google search box and look at the results. Pay particular attention to the first page of results. Research has shown that 96% of clicks occur on those first 10 links.[31] But don't stop there – you need to take a full inventory of the available online information about you. Knowledge is power, as they say, and before you can begin correcting any issues, you have to know about them.

While Google gets 66% of all Internet searches around the world, that still leaves 34% unaccounted for.[32] To be really thorough, you need to do searches on each of the two next biggest competitors as well – Yahoo! and Bing. You should also do a people search on a website such as Intelius or Spokeo, which specialize in finding information about people by crawling social media sites, government databases and more, and then aggregating that information. Typically, they sell the results; so you may not be able to verify that they have the specific information that they claim to (without paying for it), but at least you'll know what they claim to have.

Also, remember that what you may find acceptable others may not. Ask a friend with a different background from yours to pretend that he or she is an employer. Ask them to point out anything that they think could even possibly be problematic. You don't necessarily have to agree and remove the content, but it is better to know about it than not.

2. Clean up Your Accounts and Content

It's possible that, having read up to this point, when you look at the content that you have posted to sites that you control, there may be some that you would now choose to remove. Compare the content that you currently have up online with the guidelines that you established for yourself in the previous chapter. If there is any incongruence, now is the time to correct it.

Start with your Facebook account. Read the profile information that you have provided. Look at the pages that you've "liked" and any other pages that are associated with your account. Look through all of your photos and videos. Change or remove anything that you think should not be up there.

Perform the same thoughtful and thorough process on your blog, your YouTube account, your Twitter account, and any other sites where you share content.

3. Update Your Privacy Settings

Sites such as Twitter, Blogger and YouTube have fairly simple privacy controls – your content is basically either public or private to the people you select; so you can simply consider the nature of the content you are posting on those sites and choose the appropriate option.

Facebook and Google+ have more sophisticated sharing options. These sites allow you to separate your contacts into groups and share specified content with certain groups only. Google+ calls these groups "Circles," and Facebook calls them "Lists." Because more readers will be familiar with Facebook, the following steps are specific to Facebook, but the same type of process may certainly be applied to Google+ and any other sites with similar privacy options.

The first step is very basic. It's unfriend time. You need to go through all of your friends (accessible via your friend list on your profile page), and see if there are any whom you don't recognize. If you visit their profile and still don't recognize them, you need to click "Unfriend" at the bottom left of their profile page. An alarming number of students are Facebook friends with people whom they don't actually know. The account may have been created by someone to covertly learn more about you, an identity thief, or any number of other people with malicious intent. A recent study conducted by Sophos Security reported that 46% of Facebook users are willing to accept a friend request from someone whom they don't know at all.[33] Don't assume that just because you have mutual friends that those friends actually know the person – they may be part of that 46%.

Now that your Facebook friends are all people whom you actually know, we can turn back to creating lists. After logging in from the main homepage, click on "Friends" in the list on the upper-left corner of the page under your profile picture. At the top of the Friends page will be a button called "Manage Friend List." Click on that button and you will be directed to a page that lists all of your Facebook friends.

When you click on "+ Create a List" at the top of the page, a pop-in will appear that asks you to choose a name for your new list and select members from among your entire list of contacts. I recommend creating four groups: Friends, Family, Professional Contacts and Acquaintances.

Once you have created those groups, the next step is to decide which content you want each of them to be able to see. Take a look at your profile page. Every piece of content now has a little cog symbol associated with it. That is the privacy settings symbol and allows you to set the visibility of that piece of content. Sometimes, in order to see the cog symbol, you will first need to first press the "edit" button associated with that piece of profile content.

When you click on the cog symbol, you have the option to make the associated piece of content "Public," visible to all of your Facebook friends, visible just to you, or some customized group of friends. If you select custom, you can enter the names of specific people, or the name of a list that you have created. By creating a list, you can save yourself a considerable amount of time compared to entering all of those names individually.   Go through all of the pieces of content associated with your profile and decide who should be able to see which pieces.

The Privacy Settings page also has a separate area where you can control the way that other people are able to connect with you on Facebook. If you don't want to come up in the results when people search for your name, or you don't want people to be able to message you, and so on, you can make those selections there.

Most recently, Facebook has released a feature that allows you to approve the items you are tagged in. Facebook explains, "Now you can choose to approve or reject photos and other posts people tag you in before they appear on your profile. To turn this on, go to the Manage How Tags Work section of your privacy settings and turn on Profile Review." Finally, you don't have to rush to your computer every time someone puts up a new photo and tags you in it, hoping that it's not embarrassing in some way. This is a valuable tool that allows you much more control over the way that you are presented online – be sure to utilize it.

Facebook has also recently released the ability to retroactively change the privacy settings on old posts that you've made. This means that, rather than having to go through all of your old posts from months or years ago individually, you can limit their access in one quick click of a button. In your Privacy Settings, select "Limit the Audience for Past Posts." A pop-in will appear, and, if you press "Limit Old Posts," all of the wall posts you've made in the past and that have been shared with more than just your friends (e.g., public posts) will be visible to only your Facebook friends.

Finally, once you have cleaned up your profile, it is probably a good idea to double-check it by viewing it as though you were an outsider. This is similar to the "Google Yourself" step that you have already completed. Facebook offers a "View As" tool that allows you to see what your profile looks like to the public, or to a specific person. To find this tool, go to your profile and click "Edit Profile" in the top right corner. Then click "View As" in the top right corner of the editing page.

4. Ask for Content to Be Removed

Presumably, if you find content that you don't like– be it something embarrassing, personal, vulgar, false, or negative in some other way – you'd prefer that it be removed. The first step in that process is to ask.

If your friend posted the material, it should be easy enough to ask him or her to remove it. If not, finding the site's contact information may be tougher, but the process is described below. Either way, a straightforward approach, stating your preference that the content be removed and, if applicable, explaining your objection to it being online, is generally the best way to go about making the request. A good friend will understand and remove it immediately. If the friend doesn't understand, be a good friend yourself, and lend them a copy of this book.

As previously discussed, websites generally have no particular obligation to remove content just because you don't like it – even if you believe that it is defamatory. But that doesn't always mean that they won't remove it; so you might as well ask. I can tell you, based on the hundreds of take-down requests that we received at JuicyCampus, being kind, reasonable and sincere will be much more effective than being mean, threatening or aggressive. Additionally, if you are particularly vicious or crazy (and sometimes even if not), some sites will post your take-down request online, drawing even more attention to the content that you were trying to remove.

Most people-search websites have an opt-out option of which you may take advantage. If you would prefer that they not aggregate and sell your information, find the "Privacy" or "Opt-Out" page on the site, and put in your request.

Most other sites have a "Contact Us" page, or an "About Us" page that lists an email address or mailing address where you can reach the webmaster. If not, you can also try the Terms and Conditions of the site, as they generally provide at least an address where you can send legal notices. Often though, the best way to reach the owner of a particular website is to use the WHOIS database. As GoDaddy.com explains:

> The WHOIS database is a searchable list of every single domain currently registered in the world. To find out who owns a particular domain name, all you have to do is type it into the box above.

The Internet Corporation of Assigned Names and Numbers (ICANN) requires accredited registrars like GoDaddy.com to publish the registrant's contact information, domain creation and expiration dates and other information in the WHOIS listing as soon as a domain is registered.

You can go to who.godaddy.com, type in the domain name and often find the appropriate contact information for the site owner. Sometimes the owner will have used a private domain registration tool that hides the owner's information, and instead provides a proxy address through which email is forwarded.

There are very few materials that websites are legally required to remove, but one type that might apply to you is copyrighted material. The Digital Millennium Copyright Act (DMCA) requires websites to provide a DMCA contact (check for an "Intellectual Property" or "DMCA Agent" page if not in the site's Terms and Conditions), as well as a reasonable process by which copyright owners can request the removal of their copyrighted materials. Of course, this requires that you be the owner of the copyright on the material that you want removed (e.g., you took the picture or video, or you wrote the words).

5. Update and Strengthen Your Passwords

Your passwords should not be given out. Only you should have access to the content that will bear your name and affect your reputation. For example, all too often on college campuses, students will think that it is funny to log in to a friend's Facebook account and make inappropriate or awkward status updates, or comments to that person's friends and family. This creates a headache for the student whose account was used, and, depending on who sees the content, it may have lasting effects, all of which could have been easily avoided.

A strong password contains a mix of uppercase and lowercase letters, along with at least one symbol (*,&,$,%, etc.). Passwords that you use often, and that provide access to credit cards or payment tools (your online bank account, Paypal, Amazon, etc.) or that would allow a user to easily impersonate you (your blog, your email, Facebook, etc.), should be changed at least every six months. Also, don't use the same password for every site – try changing it up, perhaps even just by doing something as simple as adding the second letter of the site's name to the end of your standard password. Finally, and most important, your passwords should not be shared. If you are in a situation that requires you to share your password, be sure to change it as soon thereafter as possible.

6. Set Up a Google Alert for Your Name

A "Google Alert" is a free tool offered by Google at www. google.com/alerts. You provide Google with a key term and Google will email you to let you know about any new results that it finds that use that same term. Setting one up for your name, and for any common misspellings of your name, are good ways to keep on top of any new online content associated with your name, without having to do a search every day and look for differences.

7. Claim Your Name

If someone is able to impersonate you credibly and then create content that portrays you in a false or unflattering light, you have a problem. It can also be a problem if someone with the same name as you starts getting bad press or creating negative digital content.

One way to protect against this is to register your name as a username on all of the most popular sites that allow profiles or user-generated content. Facebook, Twitter, and YouTube are obvious examples, but what about Reddit, Flickr and Hulu, or more obscure but still popular FriendFeed, TripIt and UStream? By securing your name as a username, you make it harder for someone else to make you look bad. You can use NameGrab.com to get a list of recommended sites to put usernames on (there are more than 80), and if you don't have time to do it yourself, they'll do it for you (currently $99 per year).

Along the same lines, if it is available, you should probably register your name's .com domain (e.g., www.John-Doe.com). You can do this for about $10/year via simple services like GoDaddy.com. You don't have to build a website on it, but, if you do, it will likely have high prevalence in the search results for your name (which is important, as we'll discuss next).

LONG-TERM WAYS TO MANAGE YOUR REPUTATION

If there is still content about you online that you don't like, and the author and hosting website have declined your request for its removal, you are basically left with two options –

sue or bury. I will describe both options briefly here, but, if you elect to go this route, you will likely need additional resources and/or the help of professionals.

LEGAL OPTIONS

The right to freedom of speech is one of the most cherished values in our American society. All too often, though, people misinterpret freedom of speech as the right to say whatever they want. The law, however, actually does place several limits on speech, with the hope of protecting us. Many people have heard the example that you can't (falsely) yell "fire" in a crowded theater. In fact, the US Supreme Court has stated that, "Speech can be prosecuted if it is directed to and likely to incite imminent lawless action...."[34]

Less commonly understood, and more relevant to online reputation management, are issues of defamation, invasion of privacy, and rights of publicity. I asked Kit Winter, an expert in Internet and First Amendment law at Dykema Gossett, LLP, to explain:

> Rights regarding reputation, privacy and publicity arise under state law; so they differ from jurisdiction to jurisdiction. That said, most states have similar laws regarding defamation, which is the publication (or re-publication) of false and derogatory information about another person, whether in the form of speech (which is called slander) or writing (which is called libel). In order to constitute defamation, a statement has to involve a false statement of fact. Statements that are obviously not intended to be understood as factual– like jokes, opinions or extreme hy-

perbole – are unlikely to be defamatory (although the line between statements of fact and opinion can be surprisingly hazy). If you are a public figure, like a politician, false and derogatory statements about you are not defamatory unless they're made with knowledge or reckless disregard of the falsity, which is a difficult standard to prove. Truth is always a defense to defamation, which can be a trap for the unwary – if you sue someone for making a false statement about, for example, your sexual conduct, the person you sue may be able to inquire into your sexual conduct in order to defend him/herself! In addition, filing a lawsuit for defamation often has the unwanted result of giving even more publicity to the defamatory statements.

The right of publicity is the right to control the commercial exploitation of your name and likeness, and is recognized by most states. In general, someone cannot use your picture, name or voice to sell a product or service without your permission. If a website uses your profile picture in a banner ad, you may have a claim for misappropriation of right of publicity (unless the site's terms and conditions allow it to do this!).

Rights of privacy vary widely from state to state. A few states recognize claims for "false light" invasion of privacy, which occurs when someone makes a false implication about you (rather than a false factual statement). If someone writes an article about the rise of alcoholism on campus and puts a picture of you napping on the quad next to it, you may have a claim for false light. Most relevant to defending your reputation online, some states recognize claims for publication of private facts which allow you to sue if someone publishes personal information about you (even if it's true) where such publication would be highly offensive to a reasonable person. Like suing for defamation, suing for publication of private facts is a double-edged sword, because it requires you to admit (at least in the context of the lawsuit) that the fact is true.

If the online content you dislike seems as though it might fall into one of those categories, you may want to consider a lawsuit. Depending on the urgency (if you want it down ASAP, skip this step), the first step is probably to notify the author of the content, or the website hosting it, that you believe the content to be illegal, and once again request that it be removed. Be kind in your request. Don't be demanding. Don't threaten anyone. Just state your request, your reasoning, and then let the host know that if it is not removed within a reasonable amount of time, you will be contacting a lawyer to pursue legal action.

The good thing about making the request again yourself is that it doesn't cost anything. The bad thing is that it is rarely fruitful. Still, it is probably worth asking.

The next step is contacting a lawyer. A good Internet lawyer can cost you $300 to $600 per hour; so this is not a cheap endeavor. The first meeting, though, is generally free. A good lawyer should be able to tell you whether you have a real case, and how much pursuing it is likely to cost you. At that point, you'll have to consider how much the removal of this content is really worth to you. Sometimes a strongly worded letter from a lawyer will be enough – most websites would rather just remove a piece of content than deal with the potential cost of defending it. Pursuing a defamation case in court, however, might start at somewhere as high as $10,000.

If you lose your case, you will have paid quite a bit of money and you still can't force the content to be removed. If you win, the author of the content may have to pay damages, possibly including your legal fees. Moveover, you can prove to the website that the content is illegal, and the site will then be required to remove it, lest the site become liable as well. The whole process can take months, possibly years, so don't expect a lawyer to be a quick-and-easy fix.

PUTTING YOUR BEST SEARCH RESULTS FORWARD

Sometimes you won't be able to get rid of the content that you don't like. It's just not always possible. Maybe the content isn't illegal, just really mean. Or perhaps the content is true, but something you would rather have forgotten, or would rather keep private. You still have another option. You can bury it. You can make it so hard to find that it might as well be gone. Unfortunately, like suing, this isn't a particularly easy process. And depending on the severity of the problem, it may not be particularly inexpensive either.

You should note that, even if there aren't any negative pieces of content that you are trying to bury at the moment, the following advice can still be immensely useful – don't stop reading. Taking a proactive approach now can make it much harder for negative content to be noticed should it arise later. It can also be used to create a positive first impression on would-be searchers. Remember our discussion about First Impression Bias? People weigh the information that they find out about you first more heavily than the information that they learn later. You can use that fact to your advantage. You can have a serious and positive impact on your reputation by controlling the top results that show up on the major search engines.

The idea is simple. You want as much positive (and even neutral) content about you as possible to be online. Then, you want to make sure that content shows up before anything else in the search results.

The first step is to create, and to ask your friends and family to create, as much positive and neutral online content about you as possible. If you don't already have a Facebook, LinkedIn, Twitter, and YouTube account, it's time to get one. These services all rank very highly in search results, and allow you complete control of the content that you are presenting. You don't want to be obnoxiously overt about it, but you can use these to tastefully show off how smart, creative, and communicative you are. You should also post a generic, but positive, bio on the many profile sites that exist. Sites like PeoplePond and Spoke allow you to create profiles and link to other positive content.

Next, if you don't have one already, consider creating a personal blog. If you use your actual name as the domain name (e.g., www.JohnDoe.com), your blog is likely to be one of the first results that comes up when someone Googles your name. Services like Blogger, WordPress, Tumblr and others have made creating a blog incredibly easy. You can post things that you know will make you look good when a potential employer, date, professor, or anyone else decides to Google your name.

Once you have a good amount of positive and neutral content associated with your name online, it's time to get that content to the top of the Google search results. Google's, and other search engines', ranking algorithms are very complex, factoring in things like number of clicks that the result gets, and the frequency with which the site is updated. By far the biggest factor in the ranking, though, is the number of related links that the particular piece of content has coming from other high-quality sites. Therefore, cross-linking your content is a crucial part of getting it to show up higher in the search results. Your Facebook page should have a link to your personal blog and your Twitter account. Your personal blog should have a link to that article about you doing charity work, and the profile your friend did about you as the leader of an on-campus club, and so on.

Getting the results you want on top actually to appear there is tough. Plus, if Google detects that you are trying to game the system, it may just remove the result entirely. Search engine optimization (SEO) is a subject that many 200+ page books have been written about, and SEO companies charge their clients thousands of dollars to help with this sort of thing. If this all seems a bit overwhelming, you might want to consider getting professional help. There are a few services that will help you build and maintain a positive online image. The most prominent one today is Reputation.com. The company offers a variety of tools and services to help you monitor your online image, and also to help improve it. Recently, it even launched a product aimed specifically at students called MyReputation Student. You should research and find the best option for you, but this might be a good place to start.

CHAPTER 7: KEY TAKEAWAYS

– There are several steps that you can take today to proactively manage your online reputation: Google Yourself, Clean up Your Accounts and Content, Update Your Privacy Settings, Ask for Content to be Removed, Update and Strengthen Your Passwords, Set Up a Google Alert for Your Name, and Claim Your Name.

– If you find yourself with inaccurate Google results, one strategy is to pursue legal options. If your search contains unfavorable information about you, try managing the search results through SEO.

CHAPTER 8

A Webcam, Twitter and Tragedy

"I was shocked and saddened by the deaths of several young people who were bullied and taunted for being gay, and who ultimately took their own lives... It's something that just shouldn't happen in this country."
President Barack Obama

For most college freshmen, New Student Orientation (NSO) marks the transition from high school and living at home to the independence of adult life. During NSO, they can take a tour of the new campus, explore the surrounding city area, and meet their classmates. One of the most enjoyable parts about the first few days of freshman year is hanging out with new friends in the dormitories, chatting late into the night about everything from dining hall food to moral philosophy. And one of the most common topics of these conversations, in colleges across the country, is roommates: freshmen tell stories about their first impressions of their roommates and have fun speculating about how the next year living with them will be. They might, for example, say:

"My roommate is so shy, definitely not a party girl!"

"You're lucky; my roommate plays super loud music and always brings his girlfriend over!"

Todd Cooper (name changed), a freshman at Rutgers University who likes break-dancing and playing ultimate frisbee, talked about his new roommate, too; he posted on Twitter in late August to update his friends back home:

"Found out my roommate is gay."[35]

According to his friends, who waited eagerly for more online updates about his roommate's romantic life, Todd is not homophobic or closed-minded. One month later, on September 19th, 2010, Todd tweeted again:

"Roommate asked for the room till midnight. I went into [Maggie]'s room and turned on my webcam. I saw him making out with a dude. Yay."[36]

Maggie Jones (name changed), Todd's friend from high school who lived down the hall in the same dormitory, had allowed Todd to use her computer to start a video chat session with the laptop in Todd's room, in order to secretly watch his roommate, Tyler. Together, they had watched Tyler in a moment that was meant to be private.

In response to his updates, Todd's friends wrote messages on his Facebook wall such as, "Are you OK?" and "How did you manage to go back in there?"[37] apparently expressing their discomfort with the idea of having a gay roommate. These insensitive, homophobic comments were laid out for all to see, as were the Twitter posts, under the illusion that they would never be read by anyone but their intended audience.

On September 20th, Tyler read the posts on Twitter and Facebook, and found out that Todd had been watching him on camera. His personal life was being used as entertainment for not just Todd and Maggie, but unknown scores of people, without regard for his privacy or feelings. This was well beyond normal gossip about roommates. This was something new and frightening.

Tyler turned to an online gay community to ask for advice about what he should do about his situation. Members were supportive and encouraged him to talk about the issue with his roommate in addition to contacting university administrators, or even taking legal action for invasion of privacy. Tyler was hesitant, concerned that taking any kind of action against Todd might only worsen the situation if a change of roommates was not immediately possible.

On September 21st, Todd and Maggie turned on the hidden webcam in the dorm room again, trying to capture the same kind of "entertaining" footage. This time, Todd planned to broadcast the video online to any of his 148 Twitter followers who wanted to watch. He tweeted:

"Anyone with iChat, I dare you to video chat me any time during the hours of 9:30 and 12. Yes it's happening again."

That night, when Tyler discovered that Todd had prepared the hidden webcam for a second time, he told an RA and e-mailed other staff members about the problem.

The next day, September 22nd, 2010, Tyler Clementi, a freshman who just a month before was so excited to be attending Rutgers University and beginning his college experience, jumped off the George Washington Bridge, taking his own life.

On September 27th, Maggie Jones surrendered to the Rutgers police and was released on her own recognizance; she has left the University and enrolled in a 300-hour pre-trial intervention program.[38] On September 28th, Todd Cooper surrendered to the police and was released on $25,000 bail. Both were charged with invasion of privacy and transmitting a sexual encounter on the Internet. On April 20th, 2011, a grand jury indicted Todd on 15 counts, including invasion of privacy, bias intimidation, evidence tampering, and witness tampering. He faces up to 10 years in prison.

To Todd and his friends, seeing the webcam video might have seemed similar to watching a reality show like *Jersey Shore* or *The Real World*, where cast members hook up nearly every episode under the eye of a hidden camera on the ceiling of the bedroom. American pop culture thrives on voyeurism, viewing from a distance what would otherwise be private, personal.

Indeed, Todd seemed to have a habit of sharing things online about himself that most people would keep private – in previous tweets, he had talked about being "stoned" and had told friends to "suck my dick." Todd probably viewed his roommate's life as just another aspect of his own college experience that deserved to be shared online. Unfortunately, he missed the critical difference. While Todd had the right (however ill-conceived) to share his own life as much as he wanted, he had no right to share someone else's private life without permission.

Though Todd and Maggie were bright students at a prestigious university, they couldn't tell the difference between what information belonged to them and what belonged to Tyler. They used the Web to share information that wasn't theirs to share – a decision that led to Tyler Clementi's suicide and possible imprisonment for Todd. Though the event opened up a global conversation about homophobia, cyberbullying, and the consequences of misusing social media, it did so at the cost of one young man's life and another's future.

On the morning of the 21st, Tyler had posted on an online forum about the incident: , "...the fact that the people he was with saw my making out with a guy as the scandal whereas i mean come on...he was SPYING ON ME....do they see nothing wrong with this?"

In everyday college life, freshmen, as well as upperclassmen, have to navigate the fine line between private and public information. In many cases, they "see nothing wrong with" using their friends' and acquaintances' experiences as their own amusing stories to discuss, tweet, and otherwise share. Understanding how the choices you make in the digital world may affect others is every bit as important as understanding how those choices may affect you.

CHAPTER 9

Good People, Bad Behavior

"Cyberbullying is a serious, serious problem,
and we've got to figure out what to do to get this under control."
Dr. Phil on *CBS News*

Cyberbullying has received a lot of attention in the press, and with good reason: online harassment, verbal affronts, and persecution are some of the most difficult challenges young people face on the Web. But few people fully understand what it actually means. Cyberbullying is a broad topic that encompasses a number of different definitions. There are legal definitions, there are definitions in campus policies, and there are definitions used by the media and in casual conversation. Each is slightly different from the others. For example, the legal definitions vary among states, and the policy definitions differ from campus to campus. But they all basically come down to: the use of digital services and devices to cause harm to another person.

UNINTENTIONAL CYBERBULLYING

Some cyberbullying on college campuses is unintentional rather than a direct, malicious attack. By far the most common reason that content gets flagged (reported) on Facebook is simply that the subject of the content finds it unflattering. It's not that the content violates any particular Facebook rule (nudity, vulgarity, hate speech, etc.). It's just that the person would rather not have that particular piece of content shared online.

This should come as no surprise. Your online reputation is important to you, and other peoples' online reputations are important to them. Have you ever posted a picture of someone drinking alcohol or visibly drunk? In a silly costume? In a bikini? If so, it is quite possible that you yourself have been a "cyberbully" (in the broadest definition of the term) without even realizing it.

Similarly, someone might feel cyberbullied simply as the result of misinterpretation. Personal interactions involve a lot more than just the words that we say to one another. The tone of your voice and your body language are powerful communication tools that come so naturally that you probably don't think much about them. When you do think about them, though, it's clear how important they are. There is a big difference, for example, between shouting "I hate you" at someone, and saying it sarcastically while laughing. The nuances that create that distinction, though, are much harder to convey online. The text of an email or an SMS on your phone can never be as rich as an in-person experience. And emoticons (the little faces made up of colons and parentheses meant to express emotions) try to fill the gap, but fall well short of doing so. As a result, you may have cyberbullied, or felt cyberbullied, when that was not at all the intention.

CYBERBULLIES GO TO COLLEGE

Unfortunately, not all cyberbullying is unintentional, and, when it occurs, the results can be very serious. For victims, it can be more insidious than traditional bullying. Reactions can range from embarrassment and hurt feelings, to severe emotional distress, diffuse paranoia (when the cyberbullying is anonymous), and in the worst cases, suicide.

Sometimes people like to tell themselves that college students are beyond cyberbullying – that bullying gets left behind in high school, and that college students have moved past it. Having run the largest college gossip website in the country, I can tell you that they are not.

When JuicyCampus.com shut down, we had 1,000,000 unique visitors coming to the site every month, many of whom read and contributed to the site on a daily basis. *Radar Magazine* did a piece that called the site "shockingly nasty." That was an understatement. The posts named names, and they were racist, homophobic, misogynistic, vulgar, sexually explicit, deeply personal – you name the type of offense and it was there. The personal attacks were created by college students and aimed at their classmates and professors.

While JuicyCampus has shut down, there are already many competitors with popular college gossip sites. I also

believe that the landscape will become only more treach-
erous for college students. I predict (and hope that I am
wrong) that the next big thing in college gossip will be
proximity-based message boards, accessible only through
cell phone apps using GPS. These boards will allow anyone
to create a group (for example, the name of a dorm) and
then allow anyone nearby to anonymously post to and read
that dorm's continuous gossip feed.

It is clear that cyberbullies do exist on college campuses,
and often they arrive having had many years of practice in
high school and middle school.

Flaming: Online fighting, typically in the form of sending abusive
messages in a public forum with the intent enrage the recipient.

Example: Many residence halls and student groups have mailing
lists that members use to communicate with one another. Heated
arguments over issues large and small can erupt on these lists and
turn into "flame wars," especially when participants use "Reply All,"
ensuring that everyone sees the insults and accusations.

Impersonating: Pretending to be someone else by using that
person's online accounts, or by creating new accounts using that
person's identity, and then posting information or sending messages
intended to embarrass, or otherwise cause trouble for, the victim.

Example: Sometimes students will create fake Facebook accounts
for their professors, and use that account to send their classmates
inappropriate messages. More commonly, one student will be in
another student's room and take advantages of an unlocked computer to send messages that the victim would not otherwise send.

Trolling: Posting mean, annoying comments on a forum or online discussion area, often anonymously or pseudonymously, with the intent of upsetting the reader.

Example: JuicyCampus used to be a prime example of a place where trolling ran rampant. Today, other sites have taken its place. However, trolling does not occur only on gossip-specific sites; it can also be seen in the comments sections of YouTube videos, campus newspaper sites, and popular campus blogs, to name just a few.

Outing: Exposing someone's private information or secrets on the Web without permission.

Example: Students "out" each other in many different ways; sometimes unintentionally, other times not. They may, for example, reveal something about a friend's family or medical background that was shared in confidence. Student athletes have sometimes gotten in trouble with the NCAA for revealing private information about their teammates' injury statuses online, giving an unfair advantage to the recipients of that information.

Spamming: Sending unwanted messages repeatedly to others, in order to clog up their page or inbox and catch their attention.

Example: College students might open up their Facebook account to see that their Wall has been completely covered with posts in which each line is a new word: "Hi," "I," "Am," "Bored," "And," "Decided," "To," "Spam," "You." Spamming can be relatively harmless (mostly annoying) like this, or the content could be much worse: pornographic images, curse words or insults, for example. The number of posts is often so high that it takes the victim a great deal of time and effort to clean them off of his or her profile.

Polling/Superlatives: Labeling other students as the best at, or most likely to do, something.

Example: FormSpring, and certain Facebook Apps, allow you to pose questions to your friends. These questions can be about you, or others, and may result in labels such as, "Most Ghetto/Ratchet" or "Most Likely to Pass Out in a Trashcan." While these might seem entertaining, or even endearing, to the students who do the selecting, they can be very hurtful to the individuals chosen.

Mashups: Altering a piece of content in such a way as to humiliate the subject.

Example: Many college students are very talented photo and video editors. A bully might do something as simple as writing a negative caption across the bottom of a photo, or as malicious as reconstituting the photo to make the victim appear to be naked. After working hard to create the new photo, the editor typically shares it online, wanting to demonstrate his or her creativity and talent to others. Unfortunately, the end results can also be quite damaging to the victim.

WHY CYBERBULLYING STILL HAPPENS IN COLLEGE

I believe that most people are fundamentally good. People want to do the right thing, and they want to help one another. Sometimes though, their judgment drifts without their even noticing. From an outside perspective, it's easy to see that what they are doing is hurtful and wrong, but, in the moment, it may not be quite so apparent.

The gossip on JuicyCampus wasn't the same as offline gossip. It was much more vicious, even though the students doing the gossiping were the same. This is a common phenomenon when it comes to cyberbullying – otherwise kind, compassionate, intelligent people can easily become cyberbullies.

For a variety of reasons, the Internet makes it especially easy to lose sight of right and wrong, so much so that many students are living their lives as two different people – their online self and their offline self, each governed by seemingly conflicting ethical guidelines. As students spend more and more time online, increasingly connected by cell phones, iPads, and other devices, their two selves will inevitably become one. Soon, who you are online will just be who you are. The problem is that the online self can be pretty awful sometimes – saying and doing things that the offline self would never do. There are several reasons for this, which we will now explore.

ABSTRACTION

In a way, the entire Internet can be seen as a level of abstraction. Abstraction is defined as "considering apart from application to, or association with, a particular instance."[39] Basically, it is what happens when you replace something real with something that represents, but is not that real thing. Casinos use abstraction all the time. Instead of having you play with cash, they give you chips that represent money. The reason is that people will treat chips differently from money. Even though they represent the same thing, people have a harder time thinking of a $20 chip as being a $20 bill. In fact, they have a hard time thinking about what the chip really means at all, and so they become careless with it. People who would never bet

$100 in cash, find it easy to put down a $100 chip. This applies similarly to online behavior as well. Consider the example of watching movies. Most students wouldn't steal a DVD from a shelf, or sneak into a movie theater without paying. They recognize that as "wrong" according to their own moral code. Ask that same group of students whether they have ever downloaded a movie online without paying for it, and many would say that they have. They have a harder time recognizing that as "wrong."

It can be hard to recognize that a mean post to a public Facebook group is actually very similar to standing with a microphone and saying the same thing in the quad to hundreds of students. As a result, cyberbullying is easier to do, and doesn't feel as wrong to the perpetrator.

INVISIBLE IMPACT

It used to be that insults were told to someone's face. Consider a student, let's call her Kim, telling another student, Lindsay, that she's ugly (you can imagine a more colorful insult if you so choose). When Kim does that, she sees Lindsay's reaction – perhaps Lindsay starts tearing up, or there is a quiver in her voice when she responds. Kim recognizes Lindsay's reaction and immediately knows that she has hurt Lindsay. Unless Kim is a sociopath, something is triggered within her – her natural human instinct to look out for, not hurt, others. Suddenly, Kim feels bad about what she has done. Maybe later Kim even apologizes to Lindsay.

The Internet doesn't afford us that same luxury – we don't get those emotional cues. If you have an argument with someone online, you don't see the other person becoming upset. You aren't privy to all the non-text cues (verbal cues, body language, etc.) that remind you of the other person's humanity, and your own. And in the case of one-way harassment (posting gossip to message boards, or sharing embarrassing photos online), you don't even get the text cues. After a while, your online actions can become so dissociated from their real-life consequences that you might not even realize that you are having an impact at all. Meanwhile, your victims are still suffering the consequences.

SHAMING

For centuries, people have used shame as a deterrent against immoral behavior. In the offline world, shame may be doled out in a broad range of ways. If you see someone litter, you might glare at them as you walk by. If you catch someone cheating during a test, you might call attention to them in front of all of their classmates and the professor. And when you do these things, you may feel completely justified – from your perspective, the other person deserves to feel bad or be embarrassed. By punishing the behavior through shaming, you are decreasing the likelihood that it will happen again and sending out a warning to others who might consider participating in the same behavior. This is an important way that social norms are created.

In his book, *The Future of Reputation*, Daniel Solove notes that this same type of behavior may be seen online. The Internet allows all kinds of people to act as "norm police," enforcing social rules and punishing offenders through public embarrassment and labeling. Solove refers to online shaming as the giving of a "Digital Scarlet Letter,"[40] and he points out that there is a big difference between online and offline shaming. The Internet magnifies and prolongs the intensity of the shaming process, and as a result, the punishment often doesn't fit the crime – it is much more severe than it would be offline.

This is largely because of a hidden information problem. Individuals feel completely justified in doing a little bit of harm to someone, but they have no idea who else is doing the same thing. Collectively, their actions might be causing a lot of harm.

ANONYMITY

In some ways, online anonymity enhances freedom of speech by giving people more autonomy to express themselves than they have in the physical world. For example, thousands of people use anonymity to join support groups for diseases and other health issues, or online communities centered on unusual interests that their friends and family might otherwise judge them harshly for having.

Moreover, anonymity has the power to be a beautiful, equalizing force online. Anonymity eliminates reader consideration of factors such as race, gender, and age, making unfair discrimination impossible. Readers, therefore, have no choice but to judge only the content of the writer's message. Most people would agree that is a good thing.

However, many people also believe that online anonymity gives them a license to behave badly and without fear of consequences. Some psychologists have found that the average person, when given the ability to be anonymous, would take the opportunity to do mostly bad things, outside their normal routine, and to do so without remorse.[41] Quoting his colleague Dr. John Suler, Dr. Elias Aboujaoude explains the common rationalization for this behavior in the following way:

> Anonymity can make it possible for people to "convince themselves that those behaviors 'aren't me at all,'" ... [and if] they "aren't me," it follows that they don't reflect on me and that I'm not responsible for the consequences. This gives us carte blanche to engage in them with more abandon.[42]

This psychological phenomenon is sometimes referred to as "online disinhibition effect," which means, not surprisingly, that people lose some of their social inhibitions when they go online.[43] Have you ever noticed that most of the comments posted below a YouTube video are negative and insulting to the person who posted the video, instead of supportive? In a face-to-face environment, people tend to be more polite and positive, because social norms dictate a certain standard of how we are to treat people we engage with. But the "disinhibition effect" that occurs as a result of online anonymity often brings out both negativity and widespread criticism. Because of anonymity, people feel less accountable for what they say – and the quality of the dialogue quickly degenerates, often resulting in YouTube threads or blog comments that focus more on defamation and insults than on any thoughtful or considerate reflection.

However, those responsible for maintaining social order inside online discussion spaces have found some ways to combat these effects. One reporter writes about a community manager whose strategy is to remind users that their comments may be heard in the real world and may be harmful:

> Every once in a while, however, the mood would get "very ugly" and she would try to calm things down and remonstrate with people. "I would occasionally email them – they had to give their email addresses when registering for the site – to say, 'Even though you are not writing under your real name, people can hear you.'" In those instances, strangely, she suggests, most people were incredibly contrite when contacted. It was like they had forgotten who they were. "They would send messages back saying, 'Oh, I'm so sorry', not even using the excuse of having a bad day or anything like that. It is so much to do with anonymity..."[44]

IT'S JUST THE NORM

You probably behave differently in a classroom than you do at a bar, and at a movie theater versus a hockey game. Different places have their own well-established social norms that dictate what is and is not acceptable. The

Internet is the same in that regard. You probably interact very differently when using your work email versus your personal email, or when visiting a sports message board compared to a classroom message board.

Unfortunately, there are sites online where the social norm is to be mean. Often that meanness is considered funny, and the meaner you are, the more attention you get. Reddit, a popular content sharing tool, for example, has a whole group dedicated to misogyny. One misogynistic comment is made, and then users build on it, almost competing to see who can be more offensive. In that context, those comments may seem normal, and to some, even funny. When it feels like everyone else is doing it, it can be hard to step back and recognize that you are actually behaving in a way that conflicts with your true values – in a way that you never would offline.

ADVICE FOR CYBERBULLIES

As the previous sections make clear, it's easy to fall into behaviors online that, when you take a moment to step back and reflect on them, you realize that they don't reflect the type of person that you want to be. If you've read the previous sections of this chapter and realized that you have been a part of cyberbullying, whether inadvertently or not, this is a good time to reflect on those behaviors and consider ending them. As we've previously discussed, and as the example of Tyler Clementi and Todd Cooper powerfully illustrates, your actions may have a serious and lasting impact on you and others.

The term "anonymous" is commonly misunderstood as including "untraceable." All "anonymous" really means, though, is that your actions/comments/postings are unattributed – you don't have to sign your name next to them. A student at Loyola Marymount University found this out the hard way when he posted an anonymous shooting threat to JuicyCampus. Within hours, the police department had called me with a warrant that demanded the IP address (a unique number associated with every Internet-connected device) of the computer that made the post. A few hours after that, the student was arrested and charged with a felony. JuicyCampus was not unique in keeping a record of IP addresses. All websites must capture your IP address in order to make their sites available to you, and almost all of them maintain a record of those IP addresses. Just because you say or do something anonymously online does not mean that no one will ever know that you did it.

You should also know that all states have laws against harassment, and those laws can be (and have been) used to prosecute or punish people who use the Internet as a medium for harassment. In addition, states are increasingly amending their laws to explicitly address threatening, harassing or bullying conduct online. As of 2011, more than two-thirds of states have enacted laws that explicitly prohibit cyberstalking, cyberharassment, and/or cyber-bullying. These laws may impose criminal as well as civil liability. In California, for example, threatening to harm someone over the Internet can result in up to a year in prison. (Cal. Penal Code 422.) In Arizona, it is illegal, even for another minor, to send or possess an electronic message that includes sexually explicit images of a minor. (Ariz. Rev. Stat. 8-309.) And in Utah, it is a crime to make an electronic communication with the intent to "annoy, alarm, intimidate, offend, abuse, threaten, harass, frighten, or disrupt..." (Utah Code 76-9-201.)

ADVICE FOR VICTIMS

It's hard to know what to do when you feel like you are being cyberbullied. The first and most important thing to know, though, is that it is never really as bad as it seems at the time. It may seem as though no one understands, no one can help, and it's going to continue forever. They do, they can, and it won't; so first, just take a breath and know that things will get better. Each situation is different, and requires a unique approach, but the following basic guidelines should apply to most situations.

Consider the intent. If the person harassing you is your friend, or is a friend of a friend, or if you think there is any reason that the person may not be intentionally trying to cause you harm, there may be an alternate explanation for his or her behavior. Is it possible that you've misinterpreted what he or she has said or done? If not, is it possible that he or she may not realize the negative effect that his or her actions are having on you? Does the person consider this teasing all in good fun, without realizing that you don't? If so, you may be able to have a constructive conversation. You should consider contacting the person directly, then calmly, non-accusatorily, explaining that what they are doing is hurting you. You don't have to explain why. If it is, then that should be enough. Kindly, but directly, ask them to stop. If they decline, don't get into an argument with them. Just end the conversation.

Don't engage. If it is clear that the person cyberbullying you is doing so intentionally, it is best not to respond at all (even though it may sometimes be very tempting to). Typically, responding only makes things worse. That's what the cyberbullies want. They want to upset you, to get a reaction. By ignoring them, you deny them that satisfaction, and often, they will get bored and go away.

Keep a record. You may be embarrassed by the content that the bully is creating, whether they are messages, pictures or videos. Or you may find them so upsetting that you simply don't want them on your computer or cell phone. Avoid the temptation to hit delete. You may need to use those messages, pictures, or videos as evidence. If you don't already have them on your computer (e.g., if they were posted online, or sent to your phone), take a screenshot or picture of it (capture the message somehow).

Report it. You aren't an expert in how to deal with this stuff, and you shouldn't have to be. Report the offensive content to the website that it is occurring on (by the way, all Facebook reports are anonymous). Then also report it to a trusted family member, administrator or other authority figure. You don't have to deal with this alone.

Know the law. Specific laws vary from state to state, but, if you are being threatened or harassed, that's illegal. If you aren't sure whether your situation qualifies, just ask – local authorities (campus police, for example) are there to help. You may decide that pursuing criminal charges makes sense.

ADVICE FOR BYSTANDERS

Most college students are neither victims nor bullies; however, with newsfeeds, commenting sections, and public tweets, many students do witness some degree of cyberbullying taking place during their college careers. Some may tell themselves that it is not their problem, while others may feel powerless to do anything. It is easy to come up with a reason not to get involved, but often, standing up and speaking out can have a really strong, positive impact.

Engaging with the cyberbully online is not usually productive, and doing so may even result in your becoming their next target. But there are other ways that you may productively step in and help out. It doesn't have to be a big confrontation. If you notice that one of your friends is doing something that looks like cyberbullying to you, maybe you just casually mention (in-person) that he or she should stop. Or if you see something online that you recognize as cyberbullying, you can be the one to report it to the site. And, if you see something that's really serious, be the one to point it out to an authority figure. If your anonymity is a concern, go to someone you trust and ask him or her to keep your report confidential. Also, reaching out to the victim of the cyberbullying, offering your friendship and support, can mean a lot to that person, and make a bad situation much more bearable. Little steps such as these can make a big difference.

CHAPTER 9: KEY TAKEAWAYS

– Cyberbullying is the use of digital services and devices to cause harm to another person.

– Sometimes cyberbullying is unintentional, resulting from carelessness rather than malice.

– Cyberbullies exist on college campuses, and attack their victims in a variety of ways, including posting offensive or harassing messages to Facebook, group email lists, and anonymous message boards.

– Abstraction, invisible impact, shaming, anonymity and normality all contribute to people behaving differently (and often worse) online than they do offline.

– Cyberbullies acting anonymously are not untraceable, and they are putting their futures seriously at risk as a result of the increasing number of states passing stringent anti-cyberbullying laws.

– Victims of cyberbullying should follow five steps: consider the intent, don't engage, keep a record, report it, and know the law.

– Bystanders should proactively take steps to stop cyberbullying, whether by confronting it, reporting the behavior to an authority figure, or providing support and friendship to the victim.

CHAPTER 10

Your Digital Citizenship

"When I first saw all of these nasty comments, I did cry.
I felt like this was my fault, and I shouldn't have done this,
and this was all because of me."
Rebecca Black, singer of hit YouTube music video "Friday"

Who do you want to be online? This book has already helped to answer part of that question – considering which aspects of your personal life, professional life, and personality you want to share and with whom. But who you are online is more than just what people see in the Google search results. It's also how you choose to behave. It's the way that you treat other people, and the ethical principles that guide those interactions.

YOU'RE IN CONTROL

The digital world is only as good or bad as we make it. The Internet isn't a conscious being making its own decisions. People around the globe are contributing to its development – whether they are entrepreneurs creating new social media sites, moms writing blogs, or students using Facebook. Online social norms are still being decided, and they are being decided by you, and people like you. You have much more control than you might think.

Students on campuses across the country have organized big, successful campaigns that have fundamentally changed the way that they and their classmates treat one another online. Students at Princeton, for example, started a campaign called "Anonymity = Cowardice." Hundreds of students stood in solidarity, wearing t-shirts with the slogan, and signing an agreement not to make hurtful comments under the guise of online anonymity. Students at Emory started a campaign called "Goodbye Gossip," which asks students to pledge "speak out against discriminatory language; encourage civil discourse about topics such as sexuality, gender, race, and class status; recognize and seek to understand others' viewpoints without judgment; support those facing intolerance; and ask for support if he or she is facing intolerance."[45]

JuicyCampus had lots of visitors, but not a single consistent advertiser. The reason for this was that every time we brought a new advertiser on, students would write to that advertiser and explain the harmful impact that the site was having on their campus. Inevitably, the advertiser would remove its ads from our site. The end result was that we didn't have a sustainable business – we ran out of money, and had to shut the site down. Students played a significant role in JuicyCampus' demise.

The point is, you are powerful. You are shaping the Internet, leaving a legacy that will echo for years to come. Whether you organize a big campaign to combat issues of online incivility, actively stand up against cyberbullying or just lead the way by modeling ethical online behavior, you can have a real, lasting impact.

YOU BE THE JUDGE

No book can tell you how to be a "good" person. Life has too many gray areas. And the Internet presents even more. Ultimately, you have to decide what is right in accordance with your own personal values. So, instead of telling you what to do, or not do, below are ten tests that may help you to judge your actions and make those decisions on your own:

1. *The Golden Rule:* Are you treating others the way that you would want to be treated? Would you want to be tagged in that photo? Would you want someone saying those things about you online?

2. *The Golden Rule 2.0:* Are you treating others the way that they would want to be treated? Is it possible that they might interpret what you are doing as cyberbullying? What assumptions are you making about their comfort level with the sharing of their personal information? How are you affecting their online reputation? How well do they handle teasing? How easily do they brush off insults and let go of hurt feelings? The fact that people differ so widely can lead to reactions that you don't anticipate.

3. *The Laws and Policies Test:* Does what you are doing violate a law? Perhaps harassment, invasion of privacy, defamation, or cyberbullying? Does it violate your campus' honor code, or fundamental standard? Would you be comfortable doing this in front of a police officer or school administrator? These rules are put in place to protect people. If you are violating them, there is a good chance that what you are doing is unethical.

4. *The Everybody Test:* What if everybody is doing the same thing that you are? Would that change your mind? It may seem as though you are doing just a little bit of harm, but it's hard to know whether other people are also doing the same thing. Together, you might be doing a lot of harm, and the consequences might be much more drastic than you expected or intended. You probably don't want to be a contributor to that.

5. *The Offline Test:* What is the real-world equivalent of what you are doing? Would you be willing to do that real-world activity? Would you make that same comment to the person's face?

6. *The Real Name Test:* This test applies only to behavior that you engage in anonymously. How would you change your behavior if you knew that your real name would be associated with it? Would you still do it? Would you say it differently, perhaps more thoughtfully?

7. *The Emotion Test:* Are you doing something to someone because you are angry, jealous, or otherwise emotionally charged? Is the recipient of your actions becoming or likely to become highly emotional as a result of those actions?

8. *The Whole World Test:* Would you be comfortable with the whole world knowing what you are doing? Your family, friends, professors and professional contacts? What would the story be on the cover of *The New York Times?* Are you okay with that?

9. *The "Get It?" Test:* Is what you are trying to say hard to convey online? Is it likely to be misinterpreted? Do you have certain context that others reading it don't? If it were misinterpreted, might it be hurtful?

THE TENTH TEST

The final test is Your Test. This is the test that matters most. Consider how what you are doing reflects on you as a person. What does it say about you? Do you like what it says about you? Is the action in line with your personal values? Does it reinforce the notion of the person that you want to be?

Everyone is susceptible to errors in judgment. Everyone makes mistakes, and, unfortunately, people hurt other people. Sometimes they do it because they momentarily forget the fundamentally good person that they are, and other times they do it completely unintentionally. Your challenge now is to recognize, and avoid, the many opportunities to cause harm to others that present themselves every day online.

CHAPTER 10: KEY TAKEAWAYS

– You are in control of the Internet's future, with the potential to leave a positive impact that will last for years to come.

– No one can tell you how to be a good digital citizen, but there are several tests that might help you decide whether the behavior that you engage in online is consistent with your own values.

CHAPTER 11

The Future of Reputations

"It's taking social trust and manifesting that into
commerce... AirBnB is creating an ecosystem of trust. And now
their new Facebook implementation does it even further... It's actually
solving the trust problem as opposed to destroying it."
Ashton Kutcher

The "Sharing Economy" is a term that refers to a host
of sites and services that are reinventing the way that we
own and share physical assets. Relay Rides, for example,
is a service that allows you to rent out your car when you
aren't using it. Why not rent out your car when you are
away for the weekend, at work, or asleep? It's an easy way
to make some extra cash. But it's also risky. It's risky to let
a stranger have access to your car. And, as some users of
home-sharing website AirBnB have found, it's even riskier
to grant a stranger access to your home.

AirBnB is a website that enables people with open
couches and spare bedrooms to basically become a hotel,

renting out the space online. Since its creation in August 2008, the site has facilitated more than two million nights of bookings, at homes in more than 16,000 cities, in 186 countries.[46] Recently though, two hosts have come forward to tell their horror stories. One woman claims:

> They smashed a hole through a locked closet door, and found the passport, cash, credit card and grandmother's jewelry I had hidden inside. They took my camera, my iPod, an old laptop, and my external backup drive filled with photos, journals... my entire life. They found my birth certificate and social security card, which I believe they photocopied - using the printer/copier I kindly left out for my guests' use. They rifled through all my drawers, wore my shoes and clothes, and left my clothing crumpled up in a pile of wet, mildewing towels on the closet floor.[47]

Another man describes:

> In addition to valuables stolen, the thieves/addicts did thousands of dollars of bizarre damage to my rented home and left it littered with meth pipes. They were identity thieves, too and all my personal information was strewn about. Further investigation of my own led me to evidence that the people were not just thieves but were also dangerous. I too, feared for my own safety and would not stay at my house for some time.[48]

Obviously, this is the exception to the rule. As the CEO of AirBnB Brian Chesky put it, these actions "undermined what had been − for two million nights − a case study demonstrating that people are fundamentally good."[49] Nonetheless, it does demonstrate the importance of really knowing the identities and reputations of the people with whom you are doing business with online. There is a real need developing for an easy way to get reliable information about someone before doing business with them.

REAL IDENTITIES ONLINE

The Internet got off to a bad start. At the beginning of its existence, people were, correctly, very wary of it; so wary, in fact, that reading the headlines from news articles back then seems almost unreal. The Internet was described as a place where sexual predators created false identities and preyed on children. "Chatrooms are haven for pedophiles."[50] Anonymous trash-talkers were defaming people while lawmakers struggled to find appropriate ways to protect people from the hazards of this new technology. "House Bill might ban MySpace, Friendster."[51] It wasn't safe to use your credit card online. "Hackers get credit card numbers."[52] And you could never really trust that the person you were doing business with was reliable, or even really that person at all. "Man charged in massive eBay scam; Internet fraud case a Nashville first."[53]

That's not the Internet we know today. Things have gotten much better, and much safer, online. Now, hundreds of millions of people have online profiles, and billions of dollars are transacted online every year. That's not to say that fraud, defamation, and predation don't still occur online – certainly they do; but they aren't the first things that we think of when we think about the Internet.

This change didn't happen, and couldn't have happened, overnight. People needed time to understand the Internet better—to become more familiar and more comfortable with it. Legislators needed time to carefully think through the implications of the new digital world, and now we have seen a host of protective cyberlaws emerge. Programmers needed time to develop, test and refine their security systems, and now we don't worry about doing our banking online, or providing our social security number through the DMV website.

Over this same period of time, another important change has occurred. Educators have begun developing curricula that address the vast array of issues faced online by students today. Students, and their parents, are learning about responsible Internet use at an earlier age, thanks to organizations like Common Sense Media. Indeed, the Internet we know today is the result of the tireless efforts of thousands of thoughtful, passionate digital citizens.

Another important trend, which has had a significant impact on people's willingness to trust others online, has emerged over the past several years – the use of real identities. Randi Zuckerberg (Mark Zuckerberg's sister, and social media expert) recently commented, "I think anonymity on the Internet has to go away. People behave a lot better when they have their real names down."[54] While I'm not sure that anonymity needs to "go away" entirely – surely there is a beneficial place for it online – I do believe that there are tremendous benefits to be had as we continue to develop systems that verify and utilize real identities online.

Of course, Facebook has had a lot to do with enabling the use of real identities. While creating a fake profile page is still possible, Facebook's systems are becoming increasingly adept at detecting fake pages. And Facebook Connect allows you to log in to other sites as yourself, verified through Facebook's system. But all of this is just the beginning.

The true real identity movement will occur when we begin to see the aggregation of information from all of the sites that you use come together to create not only a verified identity, but a robust, data-based, reputation. This means involving many non-social media companies as well. Your online bank account, for example, probably required that you provide a driver's license, a social security number, and all sorts of other information to verify your identity. As a result, banks can verify your identity, plus, with your account information, they can give a measure of your financial health. Ecommerce sites have developed elaborate systems for rating buyers and sellers. Consider the fact that there are sellers on eBay today that have completed more transactions individually than eBay facilitated during its entire first year.[55] Peer-to-peer transactions online, like the host/guest relationships on AirBnB, are also on the rise. At the end of those interactions, the owners and the renters both rate one another.

In the not-too-distant future, you'll have a score, backed up by real, offline experiences, of how messy, punctual, reliable and trustworthy you are – all available in one massive, interconnected system online. Already, sites like

Klout are scratching the surface. You enter your Twitter and Facebook logins, and they give you a score based on their analysis of how "influential" you are. Soon, a company will do for your reputation what mint.com did for your finances – it will allow you to connect your LinkedIn reviews, your credit history, your eBay transaction ratings and your AirBnB guest ratings to paint a picture of who you are.

The Internet, then, will act as a powerful deterrent to bad behavior, with the potential to encourage people to treat one another better, online and off, because their online reputations will matter so much. No one wants to do business with a seller on eBay who has negative transaction feedback, and no one will want to do business with a person who has negative reputation feedback either.

EMBRACE THE CHANGE

The aim of this book has been to turn you into a conscious creator of content – someone who considers the potential consequences, for both yourself and others, every time that you update, upload, post or publish. My hope is that, having read this book, you have gained a deeper understanding of the complex issues surrounding life on today's college campus, and feel prepared to tackle those issues thoughtfully and with decency. We have discussed the fundamental differences between the online and offline worlds. We have looked at how the impression that you make online might be perceived by others, and the potential consequences of making a bad impression. I have offered some short-term and long-term strategies for managing your online reputation. We have also examined the issue of cyberbullying, and you have considered the question of what being a good digital citizen means to you. In some cases, we have focused on the negative, and worst-case, scenarios. That approach has not been meant as a scare tactic, or in any way to deter you from using technology, but rather as part of what I believe is a prudent "hope for the best, but prepare for the worst" mentality.

The best advice that I can give you today is to embrace the change that is coming. Your online reputation will increasingly affect your life. Don't just avoid having a bad one, but begin actively building a good one. Treat your peers with decency and respect, both online and off. When you notice that they're behaving with questionable judgment, don't ignore it – say something. It takes everyone's active involvement to ensure that the Internet becomes a tool that fosters good behavior, rather than enabling bad.

This is an exciting time to be a student, and an important time in the history of digital citizenship. I'm confident that you and your peers will navigate your journey through college and beyond, thoughtfully and responsibly.

Resources

Reclaim Privacy A free tool that lets you know how well your Facebook settings are protecting your privacy.
http://www.reclaimprivacy.org

Working to Halt Online Abuse (WHOA) A volunteer organization dedicated to ending online harassment and empowering victims through education. http://www.haltabuse.org

Common Sense Media An organization that advocates and provides media literacy education for families.
http://www.commonsensemedia.org/

Cyberbullying Laws A comprehensive list of cyberbullying laws categorized by state, with additional resources.
http://www.ncsl.org/default.aspx?tabid=13495

Electronic Frontier Foundation(EFF) A political advocacy organization devoted to defending civil liberties online. Includes specific sections on free speech, privacy, copyright, and other issues.
https://www.eff.org/

Social Mention A real-time search engine that tracks what people are saying about you, or a topic that interests you, across social media.
http://socialmention.com/

Notes and References

1   "Statistics," Facebook, 2011. https://www.facebook.com/press/info.
    php?statistics

2   "Writing 2.0: Free Web-based word processors," by SF Chronicle,
    CNET.com, SFGate.com, August 28, 2006. http://articles.sfgate.
    com/2006-08-28/business/17307311_1_microsoft-word-microsoft-
    office-internet-access

3   Internet World Stats, Miniwatts Marketing Group, March 31, 2011.
    http://www.Internetworldstats.com/stats.htm

4   "Current Population Survey (CPS) Internet use 2009," U.S. Depart-
    ment of Commerce, National Telecommunications and Information
    Administration, November 2009. http://www.census.gov/compendia/
    statab/2011/tables/11s1156.pdf

5   "Company," Google, 2011. http://www.google.com/about/
    corporate/company/

6   The Official Google Blog, July 25, 2008. http://googleblog.blogspot.
    com/2008/07/we-knew-web-was-big.html

7   "Mixed on Media," Insider Higher Ed News, May 13, 2011. http://
    www.insidehighered.com/news/2011/05/13/new_survey_on_
    student_technology_preferences

8 Truong, Kelly, "Student Smartphone Use Doubles; Instant Messaging Loses Favor," The Chronicle of Higher Education: Wired Campus, June 17, 2010. http://chronicle.com/blogs/wiredcampus/student-smartphone-use-doubles-instant-messaging-loses-favor/24876

9 "Section 230 Protections," Electronic Frontier Foundation. https://www.eff.org/issues/bloggers/legal/liability/230

10 "Storing Your Digital Photographs," DigicamGuides.com. http://www.digicamguides.com/store/storage-options.html

11 "Asians in the Library," uploaded by mtidd1 on March 13, 2011. http://www.youtube.com/watch?v=u7XAJo3rQn8

12 Hilton, Perez, "UCLA Girl Apologizes for Rant About Asian Students," March 15, 2011. http://perezhilton.com/2011-03-15-ucla-girl-apologizes-for-her-video-rants-about-asian-students-at-her-school

13 "UCLA Student's Racist Rant Online – David Begnaut Reports," KTLA News, March 14, 2011. http://www.ktla.com/videobeta/?watchId=cece02e7-6223-4872-877c-cfe6f2713f60

14 Oh, Soo, "Video Attacking Asian UCLA students is 'hateful and ignorant,' school chancellor says," L.A. Times Blog, March 14,2011. http://latimesblogs.latimes.com/lanow/2011/03/video-attacking-asian-ucla-students-hateful-ignorant-chancellor.html

15 Parkinson-Morgan, Kate, "Alexandra Wallace apologizes, announces she will no longer attend UCLA," Daily Bruin, March 28, 2011. http://www.dailybruin.com/index.php/blog/off_the_press/2011/03/alexandra_wallace_apologizes_announces_she_will_no_longer_attend_ucla

16 Siegler, MG, "Eric Schmidt: Every 2 Days We Create As Much Information As We Did Up to 2003," TechCrunch, August 4, 2010. http://techcrunch.com/2010/08/04/schmidt-data/

17 Klar, Yechiel, "Way beyond compare: Nonselective superiority and inferiority biases in judging randomly assigned group members relative to their peers," Journal of Experimental Social Psychology, 38,

no. 4, July 2002, pg. 331-351.

18 Curley, Shawn P., Yates, J. Frank, and Abrams, Richard A., "Psychological sources of ambiguity avoidance," *Organizational Behavior and Human Decision Processes*, 38, no. 2, October 1986, Pg. 230-256.

19 Kahneman, Daniel, and Frederick, Shane, "Representativeness revisited: Attribute Substitution in intuitive judgment," Princeton University, 2001.

20 Lorigo, L., Pan, B., Hembrooke, H., Joachims, T., Granka, L., and Gay, G., "The influence of task and gender on search and evaluation behavior using Google." *Information Processing & Management*, Vol. 42, 4. July 2006, pg 1123-1131.

21 Gladwell, Malcolm, *Blink: the power of thinking without thinking*, Little, Brown, and Company, 2005.

22 "Miss Teen USA 2007 – South Carolina answers a question," uploaded by IRamzayI, August 24, 2007. http://www.youtube.com/watch?v=lj3iNxZ8Dww

23 "Pageant Contestant Re-Answers Question," The Associated Press, The Washington Post, August 28, 2007. http://www.washingtonpost.com/wp-dyn/content/article/2007/08/28/AR2007082800734.html

24 Ibid.

25 Ito, Tiffany A., Larsen, Jeff T., Smith, N. Kyle, and Cacioppo, John T., "Negative Information Weighs More Heavily on the Brain: The Negativity Bias in Evaluative Categorizations," Journal of Personality and Social Psychology, 75, no. 4, 1998, pg. 887-900.

26 "Online Reputation in a Connected World," Cross-tab commission, Microsoft Survey, 2010. Available at http://www.marketingtecnologico.com/ad2006/adminsc1/app/marketingtecnologico/uploads/Estudos/dpd_online%20reputation%20research_overview.pdf

27 "Forty-Five Percent of Employers Use Social Networking Sites to Research Job Candidates, CareerBuilder Survey Finds," *CareerBuilder.com*, August 19, 2009.

28 Finder, Alan, "For some, online persona undermines a Résumé," *The New York Times,* June 11, 2011.

29 Ibid.

30 "Many Singles Google Potential Dates," wedlock blog, Apothic Red, February 5, 2011. Available at http://www.wedlok.com/ lasvegaswedding/dating/many_singles_google_potential_ dates-110524.html

31 Lorigo, L., Pan, B., Hembrooke, H., Joachims, T., Granka, L., and Gay, G.

32 "comScore releases June 2011 U.S. search engine rankings," comScore Press Release, July 13, 2011. Available at http://www. comscore.com/Press_Events/Press_Releases/2011/7/comScore_ Releases_June_2011_U.S._Search_Engine_Rankings

33 "Sophos Australia Facebook ID probe 2009," Naked Security, December 6, 2009. Available at http://nakedsecurity.sophos. com/2009/12/06/facebook-id-probe-2009/

34 *Brandenburg v. Ohio*, 395 U.S. Supreme Court 444, 1969.

35 "Tyler Clementi Turned to a Gay Message Forum For Help Before His Suicide," by Kashmir Hill, Forbes Blog, September 30, 2011. http://www.forbes.com/sites/kashmirhill/2010/09/30/tyler -clementi-turned-to-a-gay-message-forum-for-help-before-his-suicide/

36 "Student Who Outed Gay Roommate On Webcam Also Outed Himself On Twitter," by Andy Greenberg, Forbes Blog, September 29, 2010. http://blogs.forbes.com/andygreenberg/2010/09/29/ student-who-outed-gay-roommate-on-webcam-also-outed-himself-on- twitter/

37 Hill, K. "Tyler Clementi Turned to"

38 "Molly Wei, Defendant in Tyler Clementi Case, is Accepted Into Pretrial Intervention Program," Sue Epstein, The Star Ledger, NJ.com Blog, May 6, 2011. http://www.nj.com/news/index. ssf/2011/05/molly_wei_defendant_in_tyler_c.html

39 "Abstract," Merriam-Webster Online Dictionary. http://www. merriam-webster.com/dictionary/abstracting

40 Solove, Daniel. *The future of reputation: gossip, rumor, and privacy on the Internet*, Yale University Press, 2007.

41 Chang, Jenna, "The Role of Anonymity in Deindividuated Behavior: A Comparison of Deindividuation Theory and the Social Identity Model of Deindividuation Effects (SIDE)," *Undergraduate Journal of Baylor University*, Vol. 6, Issue 1, Fall 2008.

42 Aboujaoude, Elias. *Virtually You: The Dangerous Powers of the E-Personality*, W.W. Norton & Company, 2011.

43 Suler, J., "The Online Disinhibition Effect," *CyberPsychology and Behavior*, 2004.

44 Adams, Tim, "Internet, Anonymity, and Trolling," *The Guardian*, July 24, 2011. Available at http://www.guardian.co.uk/technology/2011/jul/24/Internet-anonymity-trolling-tim-adams

45 Friedman, Jordan, "CC, ISC Plan to Say 'Goodbye' to Gossip Site CollegeACB," *The Emory Wheel*, February 17, 2011. Available at http://www.emorywheel.com/detail.php?n=29369

46 "About," AirBnB, 2011. Available at http://www.airbnb.com/home/about

47 "Violated: a traveler's lost faith, a difficult lesson learned," by EJ, Around the World and Back Again Blog, June 29, 2011. Available at http://ejroundtheworld.blogspot.com/2011/06/violated-travelers-lost-faith-difficult.html

48 Arrington, Michael, "Another Airbnb Victim Tells His Story," TechCrunch, July 31, 2011. Available at http://techcrunch.com/2011/07/31/another-airbnb-victim-tells-his-story-there-were-meth-pipes-everywhere/

49 Chesky, Brian, "On Safety: A Word from Airbnb," TechCrunch, July 27, 2011. Available at http://techcrunch.com/2011/07/27/on-safety-a-word-from-airbnb/

50 Tinning, William, "Chatrooms are haven for paedophiles; Computer firm moves to protect children," *The Herald*, September 24, 2003.

51 Hachman, Mark, "Update: House Bill Might Ban MySpace, Friendster," *PC Magazine*, May 11, 2006.

52 Swartz, Jon, "Hackers get credit card numbers," *USA Today*, February 18, 2005.

53 "Man charged in massive eBay scam; Internet fraud case a Nashville first," *The Tennessean*, April 1, 2004.

54 Bosker, Bianca, "Facebook's Randi Zuckerberg: Anonymity Online 'Has To Go Away'," *The Huffington Post*, July 27, 2011. Available at http://www.huffingtonpost.com/2011/07/27/randi-zuckerberg-anonymity-online_n_910892.html

55 Lewis, Elen, *The EBay Phenomenon: How One Brand Taught Millions of Strangers to Trust One Another*, Marshall Cavendish Books, 2008, pg. 36.

REFERENCES

Aaker, J. L., Smith, A., & Adler, C. (2010). *The dragonfly effect: quick, effective, and powerful ways to use social media to drive social change.* San Francisco: Jossey-Bass.

Aboujaoude, E. (2011). *Virtually you: the dangerous powers of the e-personality.* New York: W. W. Norton.

Baty, K. (2011). *College safety 101: Miss independent's guide to empowerment, confidence, and staying safe.* San Francisco: Chronicle Books.

Edgington, S. M. (2011). *The parent's guide to texting, facebook, and social media: understanding the benefits and dangers of parenting in a digital world.* Dallas, Tex.: Brown Books Pub..

Fertik, M., & Thompson, D. (2010). *Wild west 2.0: how to protect and restore your online reputation on the untamed social frontier.* New York: American Management Association.

Guerry, R. (2011). *Public and permanent-the golden rule of the 21st century: straight talk about digital safety: the real consequences of digital abuse.* Indiana: Balboa Pr.

Mayfield, A. (2010). *Me and my web shadow: how to manage your reputation online.* London: A & C Black.

Myers, J. J., McCaw, D., & Hemphill, L. S. (2011). *Responding to cyber bullying: an action tool for school leaders.* Thousand Oaks, Calif.: Corwin.

Schwartz, P., & Cappello, D. (2000). *Ten talks parents must have with their children about sex and character.* New York: Hyperion.

Solove, D. J. (2007). *The future of reputation: gossip, rumor, and privacy on the Internet.* New Haven: Yale University Press.

Turkle, S. (2011). *Alone together: why we expect more from technology and less from each other.* New York: Basic Books.

Weeks, K. M. (2011). *In search of civility: confronting incivility on the college campus.* New York: Morgan James Pub.

Willard, N. (2004). *I can't see you — you can't see me: how the use of information and communication technologies can impact responsible behavior.* Eugene, OR: Center for Safe and Responsible Internet Use.

Acknowledgements

This book is the result of the efforts of a great many talented and passionate people. Thank you all for believing in this project and for helping to make it a reality. Special thanks to:

David Bohnett, for the incredible generosity of his time and talent in writing the Foreword, and for his continued support of this book and its mission to educate students;

Ed Pierce, for helping me through this process every step of the way, for his wise guidance and kind encouragement, and for contributing his impressive literary and editing talents to this effort;

Christina Farr, for providing invaluable feedback on my writing and for her thoughtful advice throughout this process;

Jennifer Aaker for her remarkable mentorship, for supporting me throughout this endeavor and for finding so many ways to be helpful without my ever having to ask;

Bill Meehan, for recognizing the importance of this topic, for his sage advice, and for connecting me with so many wonderful people;

Stephanie Parker, for her thorough research, and for her honest and intelligent feedback;

Kit Winter, for lending his expertise to provide the legal research and guidance offered in this book;

Carolyn Campbell and Kirk Mottram for their amazing help in getting the word out about this book, ensuring that it would get noticed, get read, and have the positive impact that I had hoped for;

Courtney Meehan, for contributing her expertise in digital citizenship;

Robert Denning, for believing so much in this book and for his thoughtful help all along the way;

The Stanford GSB Center for Entrepreneurial Studies, for providing its help and mentorship;

My classmates, the faculty, and the staff at the Stanford Graduate School of Business, who, in addition to inspiring me on a daily basis to create positive change in this world, helped with so many aspects of making this book possible;

And finally, for their valuable contributions in a myriad of ways: Adam Boutin, Matt Bowlsby, Nicky Colaco, Daphne Chang, Dorothy Chou, Matt Dalio, Yasemin Denari, Paul Flexton, Beth Goode, Nancy Gross, Tish Halstead, Anneke Jong, Ben Kessler, Becca Levin, Jeff Morrone, Elizabeth Mullen, Seth Norman, Ryan Pripstein, Elliot Silver, Taylor Thibodeaux, Vince Thompson, Tony Tompson, Chris Wang and Wainwright Yu.

Quote from *The Social Network* provided courtesy of Columbia Pictures.

About the Author

Matt Ivester is a technology entrepreneur born and raised in Silicon Valley. He has started a number of successful companies but is best known for having created Juicy-Campus.com, which was the largest college gossip website in the United States. Since closing down JuicyCampus, Matt has spoken on college campuses across the country covering such topics as ethical entrepreneurship, digital etiquette and online reputation management. Today, he serves as the Student Body Director of Digital Citizenship at Stanford University, where he is pursuing his Master of Business Administration with a focus on entrepreneurship. He graduated from Duke University in May 2005 with a Bachelor of Science in Computer Science and Economics.